Which way to Nineveh?

BY ETHEL BARRETT

G/L
REGAL
BOOKS
TM

A Regal Venture Book
A Division of G/L Publications
Glendale, California, U.S.A.

Over 165,000 in print

Second printing, 1970
Third Printing, 1971
Fourth Printing, 1972
Fifth Printing, 1973
© Copyright 1969 by G/L Publications
All Rights Reserved
Printed in U.S.A.

Published by
Regal Books Division, G/L Publications
Glendale, California, U.S.A.

Library of Congress Catalog Card No. 79-96703
ISBN 0-8307-0006-4

Contents

A teaching and study guide for use with this book is available from your supplier or the publisher.

Prologue

This book is a story of a nation that came apart at the seams—and got back together again.* It's a thundering story of kings and prophets and wars and spies and ambush and trickery—of bravery and cowardice—of shining honesty and outrageous mischief—and a few things more.

But it's really a story about *people*. They lived at different times and in different places, but they all had one thing in common.

They came face to face with something God wanted them to do. And they had to choose whether or not to do it. Some of them chose to do it and some of them ran in the other direction. And so each one plotted his own story by the choice he made.

Jonah was one of them and the name of that chapter is "Which Way to Nineveh?" Which is another way of saying, "Which way is God's will for my life?"

It's a good question. And you can plot the story of *your* life by the way you answer it.

*Have you read the first part of this story? You can find it in the book, "The Strangest Thing Happened . . . ," published by Regal Books, a division of Gospel Light Publications. Look in your bookstore.

CHAPTER 1

A Little Guy with a Big Problem

II Kings, Chapters 11 and 12; II Chronicles, Chapter 24

The baby boy lay in his bed in the royal nursery. The whole palace was quiet. He heard the strange and distant sounds without understanding; he did not know that they were the rumbling of wheels and the clatter of horses' hoofs on the streets outside. He did not know that he was a king's son. Or that his father was dead. Or that the distant sounds were the sounds of his father's funeral. He was in his own little world and his own little world was the palace nursery. The only problem he had in the world was how to manage his wobbly legs. He did not know that he was about to be murdered.

The World Outside

The baby's name was Joash. And to understand who he was and why he was in trouble, you have to go back in history.

1

The world outside that palace nursery was big and wide —and very very grim. The palace was in Jerusalem, the capital city of the country of Judah. Many years before, the baby's great-grandfather, the good king Jehoshaphat, had ruled the kingdom of Judah in peace. When Jehoshaphat died and his son Jehoram took over, things should have gone on very tidily, but they did not. For Jehoram had taken a bride from the northern kingdom of Israel, and *she* was the daughter of the wicked king Ahab and queen Jezebel! If you think this led to trouble, you are right; it did. Jehoram brought her down to Judah to reign with him, and between the two of them they led the kingdom of Judah away from God, into the worship of Baal, and out, as they say, on a limb.

They had a son and his name was Ahaziah, and as you might suspect, he was a rascal too. Then Jehoram died and his wife Athaliah and his son Ahaziah were left. Ahaziah took over as king.

Then Ahaziah died*—and who was to take over now?

Ah, there we have it. For one of Ahaziah's children—his youngest son—was that baby in the nursery. It was Ahaziah's funeral that was going on outside.

The Family Album

So the boy Joash lay kicking his blankets. He was the son of the wicked king Ahaziah who was the son of the wicked king Jehoram and the wicked queen Athaliah who were the children of the good king Jehoshaphat and the wicked king Ahab and queen Jezebel. What a family album! Except for

---

*He took a trip to Israel (where he had no business being in the first place) and was killed in a skirmish there. You can find the story in II Kings 9:14–29.

Jehoshaphat, color them all evil. Joash wasn't *any* color—
yet.

His life was in danger. But after all, he *did* have Queen
Athaliah to protect him. And after all, wasn't she his *grandmother?*

The Shortest Kingship in History

Athaliah was in her private quarters with her advisors.

The funeral was over. The cries of "The king is dead!"
had stopped now, and the city was quiet.

"The king is dead," said one of the advisors.

There was silence.

"Long live the king," said another, finally.

There was another silence. This time Athaliah broke it.
"Long live the *queen*," she said.

"But your grandchildren—"

"I have two ambitions," she shot back. "One is to keep
Baal as god of this people. The other is power. *Power.*"

They waited.

"And I'll do anything to get it." She stood looking out the
window for a long time. Then she turned. "I want every one
of my grandchildren killed," she said quietly. But it seemed
like a bombshell. No one spoke. "*All* of them," she said. And
this time they believed her. It was an order. Joash was
about to be murdered, his reign ended before it began. And
there seemed no way to stop it.

Or was there?

The Longest Odds in History

In the Temple in Jerusalem lived a priest, a great man of
God. His name was Jehoiada (II Chronicles 22:11). And he
had a wife. Her name was Jehosheba. She was a great
woman. She loved the living God. And she would have

3

stayed in the Temple and performed her duties and minded her business without ever getting into this story—except for one thing. She heard the ugly rumor of Athaliah's plans to murder her grandchildren. And she rose up in sheer horror. For *she was their aunt.* She decided that *something* had to be done. And quickly.

The Most Daring Kidnapping in History

We do not know exactly *how* she did it. The Bible does not give us the details. Just says she kidnapped Joash. But what a story *that* must have been!

The lone figure wrapped in a long dark cloak, slithering through the palace corridors in the dead of the night, darting into doorways at every sound, reaching the nursery— and coming face to face with the children's nurse!

The whispered conversation. One of the children had to be rescued. The heartbreaking choice. Baby Joash. He would be the easiest one to take. And the nurse must come along. She says no, terrified. "They'll kill you too," Jehosheba hisses in the darkness. "You have nothing to lose! Come!" The two of them start off, down the long long flight of marble stairs. The baby whimpers. "Put him under your cloak!" Jehosheba cries in a whisper. "Quickly!" And off they go, hiding in doorways, darting across open spaces—and at last, the Temple! They hurry in, up back stairways and finally into the quarters where Jehosheba and her husband Jehoiada live. There the nurse uncovers him and he blinks in the strange light. And his Aunt Jehosheba takes him in her arms. And rocks him gently. He is safe at last.

The Strangest Childhood in History

And what a story the next few years must have been! Joash, living secretly in the Temple, in the very shadow of the palace where his wicked grandmother was ruling! And being loved. And learning. Learning about his God.

Can you picture it? At first it's in faltering small-boy manner.

"Preserve me—"

"Oh God," Jehosheba prompts.

"Oh God. For in thee—for in thee—"

"Do I put my trust," she says.

"In thee do I put my trust!" he finishes triumphantly. He's lisping but he gets the idea.

Then the years go by—

"Thou shalt have no other gods before me," he says, and this time there is no prompting. "Thou shalt not make unto thee any graven image, or any likeness of anything that is in heaven above, or that is in the earth beneath—"*

And so it goes.

And six long years go by and he is seven years old—old enough now to understand. Can you picture it?

"It must be wonderful to be a king. And rule a country, Aunt Jehosheba."

"Wonderful, dear."

"You've taught me the history of this country so I know it backwards. And of my people."

"Yes, I know."

"If—if this country of Judah is worshiping idols and the queen is wicked, there ought to be a *good* king to come along and—take over."

"Joash, you—"

"I wish *I* were that king."

"Joash—" She leans forward, puts her hands on his shoulders. "Joash—you *are* that king."

"You—you're pretending."

"No, I'm not pretending. Listen. Listen carefully to what I'm going to tell you—"

*Deuteronomy 5:8.

And she tells him and he listens, wide-eyed, unbelieving. She tells him of his rescue and why. And she tells him of the plans that even now are being made. And she tells him of the dangerous and exciting thing that is going to happen—within a few days!

The Stage Is Set

Joash's uncle laid his plans carefully. As Temple priest he was a man of authority. And from what he did, he must have been a leader of men.

He called in the five captains who commanded the five hundred royal guards. Swore them to secrecy. Told them he needed their help. Then he told them the whole story of Joash, from his rescue on—all of it. Then he told them his plans.

The Actors Take Their Places

It all had to be done quietly and in secret. The godly leaders from all over Judah were summoned, and they sneaked into the city of Jerusalem. There they were told what to do, and there they waited for the fateful day. Every man had his orders.

The Curtain Goes Up

The fateful day was a Sabbath and it started out like any other Sabbath. The Temple area was crowded.

Then came time for the changing of the guards. But the guards who went off duty did *not* go "off duty"—they sneaked around to the Temple storehouse where they were given spears and shields that King David had stored there many years before. And they sneaked back and took their positions. The Temple area was now heavily guarded from every corner. The crowds waited. They were expecting something. But *what?*

The Drama Begins

Jehoiada came out of the Temple. With him was a small boy. The crowd watched, waited, silent. And in the silence, Jehoiada began to speak. The next few moments were stunning, unbelievable. The small boy was Joash! Joash was alive! With their mouths gaping open they watched Jehoiada put a crown on the boy's head. And give him the law of the Lord. And anoint his head with oil. And proclaim him

They stood stunned for a moment. Then, as the full realization of it hit them, they took up the cry. "Long live the king! LONG LIVE THE KING!!!!!"

And the din of the bugles and the shouting was deafening. It filled the Temple area and reached beyond—to the palace itself. Everyone in the palace heard it. The noblemen heard it. The servants heard it. They scurried about in a panic, getting stuck in doorways. Queen Athaliah heard it. Before her advisors could stop her, she rushed from the palace and headed for the Temple.

The Curtain Goes Down

She got to the edge of the crowd in the Temple court—and stopped short. There up on the steps stood a boy—with a crown on his head. It couldn't be—it wasn't possible—! They had crowned him king!

"Treason!" she screamed. She elbowed her way to the front. Her hair was loose and streaming down her back. "Treason!" she screamed again, and tore her clothes, and her face was like the face of a madwoman. "TREASON!!!"

But the armed guards were coming toward her. She backed up a few steps—and turned. There were armed guards behind her. She turned again—and began to run. No one chased her. She fled in panic out of the Temple court—toward her palace—out by the Horse Gate. But there were armed guards there too.

It was out by the Horse Gate that she was killed. The curtain went down on one of the most dramatic days in history.

Off to a Good Start

"LONG LIVE THE KING!"

Yes, Joash was saved to be king. But more important than that, the people of Judah were going to get straightened out

8

again. For it tells us in the Bible that Joash's Uncle Jehoiada "made a covenant between himself, all the people, and the king, that they should be the LORD'S people."

Yes indeed. And it was about time. (See II Chronicles 23:16, *The Amplified Bible.*)* Now, at long last, everything was going to be all right again.

Full Speed Ahead

And everything was! Joash was king, growing up under the supervision of his Uncle Jehoiada. And they were golden years.

Now when you start reforming a kingdom, some things have to be torn down. And they were. The house of Baal and all the altars.

And some things have to be built up. The most important was the Temple itself. After some delay (people sometimes need a bit of nudging) Jehoiada arranged a foolproof method.† A huge box was placed at the entrance to the Temple (you couldn't miss it) with a Temple priest standing by (you couldn't sneak by it). As the people gave the priest their offerings of silver, they watched him put them in the box. No fudging. And no nonsense.

The result?

Cedar timbers! Blocks of stone! Laborers and craftsmen! Walls repaired! The Temple beautified!

And so Joash ruled, with the advice of his uncle. And the years that followed were wonderful. Everything was full speed ahead, and on the right track—and then—Jehoiada died.

---

*"The Amplified Bible." (Grand Rapids: Zondervan Publishing House, 1965.) Used by Permission.

†If your father is on the church building-program committee you might tell him about this.

"What? I'm on My Own?"

Joash was on his own. But he was well-established now. He's had years of loving training and good example. And he had one greater than his uncle to turn to. He had God. He should do greater things than ever before. And with a lifetime of good training behind him and God to advise him, what did he do?

The Wrong Turn

He turned to his *friends*.

Oh, *No!*

Oh, *yes.* He forgot everything he'd ever been taught, and he turned to his friends for direction—and the direction turned out to be down, all down.

It's hard to believe, but he actually led his people back into the worship of Baal.

The Big Slide Down

The life of Joash is a package deal and you have to take the bad with the good, and here it is. It isn't a pretty story.

In lovingkindness God sent prophets to warn him but he would not listen. The worship of Baal continued. Down, down. Then God sent Zechariah, *the son of Jehoiada* to warn him.

And Joash had him killed. Down, down, down.

God had had enough.

The rest was shambles. From that point on, Joash's life fell into a million pieces. God allowed the Syrian army to invade Judah. The Syrians robbed Joash, and killed and plundered all over his kingdom. And then down, down, down, to rock bottom.

Joash was killed by his own servants, to avenge the death of Zechariah.

The golden days were over.

The King Who Never Grew Up

Joash was a boy who had TLC* and good training. And he made a great king—as long as he was under his uncle's supervision. But when he got out on his own he came unpasted. He had never really grown up.

What About You?

When people tell you, "Oh, grow up!"†—what do you think they mean? Think of some decisions you still have to make on your own even though you are under your parents' authority.

Of course to grow up spiritually you've got to have life to begin with. You can "come alive" in Jesus Christ by believing that He is the Son of God and accepting Him as your Lord (John 3:3; 1:12).

The Bible says that God will strengthen you and make you what you ought to be and *equip* you with everything good so you can carry out His will (Hebrews 13:20,21). But after you get your instructions the Bible tells you—"Don't just stand there—do something!" (See James 1:22.) You can never grow up without exercising your spiritual muscles. And you are being trained now for the time when you are *on your own*. When Joash was on his own, he blew the whole thing into shambles. You are being trained so you won't.

*Tender Loving Care.

†What? They don't tell you this? Well, don't be too sure they're not thinking it.

11

CHAPTER 2

Which Way to Nineveh?

The Book of Jonah

"I'll Do Anything You Say, Lord—Except—"

"Predict to the king that the country will be victorious over Syria," said the Lord.

"Yes, Lord," said the prophet.

"Tell the king I said thus and so."

"Yes, Lord."

"Now do thus and so."

"Yes, Lord."

"Now get thee up and go to Nineveh—"

"Yes, Lord?"

"And tell them to repent—"

"WHAT?"

Seems like a strange attitude for a prophet who'd been obeying God all his life without question.

The prophet's name was Jonah. And he's probably one of the best known characters in history. Everybody knows

13

Jonah. And how he got swallowed by a fish. But few people know how he got into the mess in the first place. In order to understand it you have to get back and look at the whole picture. It's a fascinating study in social studies, politics—and human nature.

"Everything's Great, Lord, Except for My Enemies"

Jonah was the prophet in Israel in those days. And Israel was prospering. Gone were the days of defeat and humiliation. Joash was dead; his son Jeroboam the second ruled in his stead. And Jeroboam the second was one of the greatest kings in the history of Israel. He'd turned the country away from Baal worship and back to God. He'd conquered nearly all of Syria (Jonah had predicted that he would). He'd made Samaria the greatest city in the land. And the country of Israel was on its way to being almost as great as it had been in the glorious years of King David! Happy days were here again!

Except for one thing.

Assyria. A huge country, off to the north, right on the border of Syria. Now it's one thing to have a powerful godly neighbor and quite another to have a powerful wicked one. Assyria was wicked—very. And most of its power and most of its wickedness was centered in its capital—Nineveh, a great city sprawling over sixty square miles, and you could color every bit of it evil. And so Assyria (and Nineveh!) lurked like a great shadow, off to the north—a constant threat to Israel's safety. Who could tell when this greedy monster would yawn—and stretch—and leap to devour?

Grim business.

And so we have a prophet (Jonah) who lived in a prosperous and godly land (Israel) and everything is going very well, thank you, when he is told to pick up his duffle bag

and get himself off to his country's worst enemy and—
what?

"What? Help My ENEMIES?"

Warn them to repent, was what. Or they'd be
overthrown. And what if they *did* repent? And if they did,
what if God saved them? Horrible thought! Why the
dearest thought in Jonah's heart was that God would *clob-
ber* them!

"I know that you're a gracious God," whined Jonah, "and
merciful. And slow to anger. And of a great kindness. If
they repent you might—you might—"

Yes indeed.

"I Want Your Will, Lord, but Not Right Now"

The busy seaport of Joppa was humming with activity.
Shouting, grumbling, laughing, the whack of the ship-
wright's mallet, the creak of pulleys hauling cargo aboard,
the squawking of parrots—

And ships. Big ones, middle-sized ones, old and dirty ones
with dirty sails—bright new ones with brilliant orange and
yellow and scarlet sails, and names of heathen gods in glit-
tering letters on their bows—

Into this commotion came Jonah. To board a ship. To go
to Nineveh? Hardly. Nineveh was hundreds of miles inland,
to the northeast. He boarded a ship to go to *Tarshish*.
Which was in the opposite direction, and one of the most
remote trading places known. It was about as far away from
Nineveh as he could get. He paid his fare, went below deck
—and went to sleep. He'd washed his hands of the whole
affair.

The ship set sail, bound for Tarshish.

"Maybe the Lord Won't Notice"

Of course the Bible tells us that we cannot run away from God. "Whither shall I flee from thy presence? If I take the wings of the morning, and dwell in the uttermost parts of the sea; even there shall thy hand lead me, and thy right hand shall hold me."* But Jonah didn't know that—not yet. He had to find out the hard way. And he was asleep when it happened.

"You've Found Me Out!"

It was a storm and it was a killer. The ship ploughed valiantly into the giant waves but they tossed it about like a matchbox. The frantic orders of the captain and the shouts of the sailors could scarcely be heard in the screaming wind.

"Cargo overboard!"

They worked frantically to lighten the ship.

And just as frantically they began to pray to their heathen gods.

But the storm grew worse.

The first Jonah knew of it, the captain was shaking him awake. "What do you mean, you sleeper? Arise, call upon your God! Perhaps the God will give a thought to us, so that we shall not perish!"†

Jonah staggered out of his bunk and went up into the blinding fury of the storm, suspecting that he had made a bad choice in starting for Tarshish. When he saw the frantic faces of the sailors, he was pretty sure of it. Then they drew

*Psalm 139:7,9,10.

†Jonah 1:6, "Amplified Bible."

lots to see whose fault the storm was. Drawing lots is the same as "drawing straws," but no matter what you call it, it was all bad. The lot fell on Jonah.

Now he knew it. He was clearly out of God's will—way out.

"Okay—I Confess"

"Who are you?"

"Where do you come from?"

"What is your occupation? Your country? Your nationality?"

The sailors' questions were screams, barely making it above the din of the storm. There was no time to quibble.

"I am a Hebrew, and I reverently fear *and* worship the Lord, the God of heaven, Who *made* the sea and the dry land."* Jonah was terrified.

"Then what can we *do* to you to appease your God and calm the storm!"

Ouch.

"Cast me into the sea," Jonah said miserably.

"I'll Take My Punishment like a Man"

You really have to give those heathen sailors credit; they behaved more like Christians than Jonah. They didn't want to throw Jonah into the sea. They took to the oars instead, for one more try. But the storm grew worse. At last they prayed in desperation to *Jonah's* God—"Let us not perish for this man's life!" But the storm grew worse. And at last they cast Jonah into the sea.

*Jonah 1:9, "Amplified Bible."

17

"God Works in Spite of Me?"

The sea grew calm. Incredibly. The sudden quiet was almost as terrifying as the storm had been. In fear and trembling, the men "reverently *and* worshipfully feared the Lord exceedingly, and they offered a sacrifice to the Lord and made vows."*

Jonah had unwittingly become a missionary.

"I've Taken My Punishment—What Now?"

Jonah's worst punishment was yet to come. You've cut your teeth on this part of the story. Jonah and the whale. We know there are whales with crushing teeth and small throats that couldn't swallow a man, and whales with large throats and bone plates instead of teeth that could, and the white whale sharks of the Mediterranean that have been known to swallow men—and horses—and once even a reindeer, and whales that have huge cavities in their heads where they put things they can't swallow—and men and animals who've been found alive days after being swallowed—

But all of this is beside the point. The Lord had prepared a great *fish* to swallow Jonah. It was a miracle, and He was quite up to it.

If you think Jonah's troubles were over, read chapter two. "You cast me into the deep, into the heart of the seas . . . the floods surrounded me. . . . Your waves and Your billows passed over me . . . I am cast out of Your presence. . . . the sea-weeds were wrapped about my head. . . ."** Three days of agony. And finally—

"I will pay that which I have vowed!"

Well it's about time.

*Jonah 1:16, "Amplified Bible."
**Jonah 2:3–5.

18

"Okay, I'll Do It, I'll DO It!"

This was precisely what God had in mind in the first place. It was only then that He caused the fish to vomit Jonah back up—on dry land. Which put Jonah right back where he'd started. "Get up and go to Nineveh," said God— "and preach what I tell you!"

This time there was no quibbling. Jonah made the weary trek inland to Nineveh—and preached. What God told him.

"Repent! Yet forty days and Nineveh shall be overthrown!"

"You Mean My ENEMIES Can Be Good Guys?"

The effect was stunning. The people on the streets believed him. They repented in sackcloth and ashes and refused to eat. The word spread all over that great city, even to the palace. And the *king* believed it. *He* repented, and issued a proclamation that every last person in Nineveh repent too, in sackcloth and ashes. Everyone fasted—they

19

didn't even feed the animals. And that great and wicked city of Nineveh stopped in its tracks as one man, and cried out to God—"Save us!" The heathen in Nineveh were quicker to obey God without question than Jonah had been. And because they obeyed, God *did* save them!

"But They've No RIGHT to Be Happy—They're ENEMIES!"

And the people rejoiced and worshiped God and there was great joy in the city. Except for Jonah. "Isn't this just what I told you back in my own country?" he wailed, "That's why I fled to Tarshish! I knew you are a gracious God. And merciful. And slow to anger. And of great kindness. I knew you'd go and do this!"*

"Do you do well to be angry?" asked God.

"Ohhhhhhh," bellowed Jonah, "I want to die!"

A real tantrum, that. Completely unreasonable.

"Okay, So I'm Sulking"

And he didn't get over it at once, either. He went outside the city, built himself a little booth and sat down to wait. Still angry.

But God wasn't finished with him yet. In one way or another, He was going to see that Jonah got the point.

First He prepared a gourd (plant) and it grew like Jack's beanstalk until it was so huge it was up over Jonah's head, sheltering it from the sun. Jonah was glad about the gourd, but still not glad about Nineveh. So the next morning God prepared a cutworm *and* a sultry east wind. The cutworm destroyed the gourd and the wind was like the heat from a

*Read Jonah 4:1–3.

blast furnace. Jonah fainted. But he still didn't get the point. "I want to die," he wailed.

"God, How Patient Can You BE?"

"Do you do well to be angry over the gourd?" said God.

"*Yes*," said Jonah, "angry enough to die."

"You have pity on a *gourd*," said God. "And shouldn't I spare Nineveh? A hundred and twenty thousand *people?* And their animals?"

Oh, the tenderness, the patience, the lovingkindness and mercy of God! Jonah must have crumpled in the dust, in tears.

He finally got the point.

He must have. For he wrote it down and the book of Jonah is here in the Bible. He didn't spare himself; he colored himself stubborn.

And did Assyria attack Israel as Jonah had feared? Of course not. Nineveh had turned to God; she was no longer an enemy!

It all could have been so simple. But Jonah made the wrong choice and learned all of it—the hard way.

"Yes Lord, Yes Lord—WHAT?"

Don't you feel silly?

When you obey God, you obey Him without question. For He says, "For my thoughts are not your thoughts, neither are your ways my ways, saith the LORD. For as the heavens are higher than the earth, so are my ways higher than your ways, and my thoughts than your thoughts."*

Do you good to memorize it.

*Isaiah 55:8,9.

21

CHAPTER 3

All for You

Isaiah Chapters 6, 40, 53

It was an experience never to be forgotten. The young man was in the Temple praying, when suddenly he saw—

The Lord Himself seated upon a throne high and lifted up, the train of His robes flowing over the Temple floor! And Seraphim* crying to one another, "Holy, holy, holy, is the Lord . . . the whole earth is full of His glory!" (Isaiah 6:3, *Amplified Bible*).

And the very foundations of the Temple seemed to shake with the voices and the Temple was filled with the glory of the Lord!

And the young man cried out in terror, "What is to become of me? I am undone! I have sinned; I dwell among people who have sinned!"

*Heavenly beings.

23

And one of the Seraphim picked up the tongs from the altar, lifted a burning coal from the fire, and touched the coal to the young man's lips.

"Now you are clean," the Seraphim said.

And then—

"Whom shall I send, and who will go for us?"

It was the voice of the Lord!

What a call! What a thundering, earth-shaking, life-spinning experience!

"Here am I," the young man said. "Send me." He was never to be the same again.

His name was Isaiah.*

Mission Impossible—Without God

His mission?

He was to spend the rest of his life, down through the reigns of three kings—warning Israel and Judah of what was to come if they did not obey God.

And he did.

But he also predicted things that would happen long after Israel was gone and Judah was gone. He predicted the birth and the life and the death of our Lord Jesus Himself.

He Would Be Born—

First Isaiah predicted His birth:

"Behold," he said, "a virgin shall conceive, and bear a son, and shall call his name Immanuel," which means "God with us."†

*Read Isaiah 6:1–8.

†Read Isaiah 7:14.

24

And Heralded by a Forerunner—

Then he predicted a forerunner for our Lord, when He was ready to begin His ministry. This was a term the Jews knew well in those days. When a king was to pass through a land, the forerunners were a very important part of his coming. They went ahead and prepared the way. The rocks were hauled out of the way, the rough places were smoothed out, the crooked places were made straight. But Isaiah wasn't talking about a road project; he was telling the Jews to prepare their hearts for the Lord's coming. How? The rocks of pride were to be hauled away, the rough places of squabbling and warring smoothed out, the crooked places of sin straightened.

"The voice of him that crieth in the wilderness," he told them. "Prepare ye the way of the Lord, make straight in the desert a highway for our God!"

And Be Rejected—

He predicted the kind of reception our Lord was going to get—both at His birth and throughout His life. And the words he used were sad ones—despised, rejected, forsaken by men, a man of sorrows, acquainted with grief, one from whom men hide their faces . . . (From Isaiah 53:1-3).

And Suffer—

He predicted that our Lord would suffer and die for *our sins*. Wounded for *our transgressions*, he said. Why? For we have gone astray like sheep, he said, we have turned every one to his own way—and God put on Him the guilt of every one of us (see Isaiah 53:4-6). And he said our Lord would do this willingly.

25

And Die—

He predicted that our Lord would be crucified with sinners. Willingly. That He would let Himself be regarded as a criminal and be numbered with the transgressors (see Isaiah 53:12, *Amplified Bible*).

All these things Isaiah said, and all these things happened....

SEVEN HUNDRED YEARS LATER

He Was Born—

The little town of Nazareth was the last place in the world where anything important would be expected to happen. It was like a basin, nestled in the southern ranges of lower Galilee. If you took a walk to the rim of the basin you could see Naboth's vineyard—and dozens of battlefields, scars of ancient Israel.

And Nazareth would have been forevermore just a spot on the map except that one day the angel Gabriel was sent there from God.

The angel Gabriel visited Nazareth specifically to visit a young girl of no particular importance, except that she was a descendant of David. Her name was Mary.

"The Lord is with you," he said, "and you are highly favored among women."

Mary looked at him in confusion. What did he mean? "Don't be afraid," he said, "You are going to have a son, and you'll call His name JESUS. He shall be great, the son of the Highest. And of His kingdom there shall be no end."

"But how? How can this thing be?" she asked, for she was engaged to a man named Joseph. A child of *God?*

"The Holy Spirit shall come upon you, and the power of the Highest shall overshadow you: *therefore also that holy* *thing which shall be born of thee shall be called the Son of God."**

It was so. The Son of God. Absolutely incredible and impossible, but it was so.

"Let it be done to me as you have said," Mary answered finally.

Whether she had any doubts about telling Joseph, we do not know. If she did, they were not for long. For an angel appeared to Joseph in a dream and told *him* not to be afraid —for Mary's baby would be the Son of God. "And thou shalt call his name JESUS," he said, "for he shall save his people from their sins."

And the Bible tells us* that this was done so Isaiah's prophecy would be fulfilled—"Behold, a virgin shall be with child, and shall bring forth a son, and they shall call his name Emmanuel, which being interpreted is, God with us."†

THIRTY YEARS LATER: THE FORERUNNER

And Was Heralded—

Who was he? His doings were the gossip of the town. Jerusalem was buzzing with wild accounts of this strange man, stalking out of the hills of Judea like another Elijah, and preaching like thunder. "Repent!" he cried, "For the kingdom of heaven is at hand!"

Thousands flocked out to the desert to hear him. And the stories flew back. His garment was of camel's hair, he wore a leather girdle about his loins, he ate nothing but locusts and wild honey. And he was baptizing people in the river Jordan. Scandalous! The gossip was the most flourishing

*See Luke 1:26–35.

†See Matthew 1:22,23.

27

within the courts of the Temple itself. The Pharisees and Sadducees wagged their heads and pulled their beards and speculated, and finally decided to go out and see for themselves. One look at *them* should shut him up.

But he did not frighten easily. "And who warned *you* to flee from the wrath to come?" he bellowed when he saw them. And before they could confront him with his scandalous acts, he gave them a lacing that left them shaken, ending with "Yes I baptize with water—but He who is coming is mightier than I—I'm not worthy to unloose the strap of His sandal!"

The gossips grew busier. Who *was* he? The Elijah? The Messiah Himself? First they buzzed it among themselves, then they came out and asked him.

"Who are you?"

"I am not the Christ," he said, reading their minds.

"Who then? Are you Elijah?"

"No."

"*Who* then?"

"I am the voice of one crying in the wilderness.* Make straight the way of the Lord!"

The next day he saw Jesus in the crowd. "Behold the Lamb of God," he said, "who taketh away the sin of the world!"

It was the beginning of a furor that lasted three years. God was with them and they didn't know it.

. . . . . .

JERUSALEM

And Suffered—

The streets of Jerusalem were in incredible confusion. The shops had been deserted. All the wares that had been

*He was John the Baptist.

28

outside the shops—fruit, meat, chickens, spices, nuts, camel's feet—had been pushed aside, trampled by the crowds. The crowds strained back to let the man through. He was stumbling under the weight of a huge wooden cross. They were making Him carry it Himself—to His own crucifixion. His name was Jesus of Nazareth. Nazareth of Galilee. They called Him the Galilean. He'd had a ministry that had upset Jerusalem and the world outside. Healing the sick, casting out demons, drawing thousands to hear His preaching, and even proclaiming that He was the Son of God.

Well now He was going to get His comeuppance.* He'd had no business doing such things and claiming such things. Outrage!

After all His high and mighty doings, He'd had quite a week. He'd been before the High Priest, before the council, before Pilate, before Herod—He'd been whipped, spat upon, crowned with thorns—and even denied by His own disciples.

And now He was being taken outside the city gates—to be crucified with criminals—two thieves of no account.

And Died—

"Crucify Him! Crucify Him!" The crowd was out of control now. Only a few hung back and wept.

And so He was taken outside the city gates and crucified on a cross. Between two thieves. His mother was there. She believed on Him. Some of His disciples were there. They believed on Him. One of the thieves believed on Him. And a Roman centurion. That was all. No one else believed. No one at all.

*Get what was coming to him.

The man was the man of sorrows Isaiah had been talking about. He was Jesus Christ our Lord.

All of Isaiah's predictions about our Lord had come true.

Was That the End?

No it wasn't. Our Lord rose from the dead. And appeared to those who loved Him, many times. The stories are great and you can read them in all the Gospels. They are too many to cover here. But the most important one took place on the top of the Mount of Olives.

He was there with His disciples after His resurrection, and before their very eyes, He ascended—out of their sight —and up into heaven. You can read about it in Mark 16:19– 20 and Luke 24:50–53. And Acts 1:9.

And He's coming again! "Why do you stand gazing into heaven?" the angels said to the disciples. "This same Jesus, Who was caught away and lifted up from among you into heaven, will return in [just] the same way in which you saw Him go into heaven" (Acts 1:11, *Amplified Bible*).

All for Me?

All for you. He was born, He died, He rose again, and He's coming back—all for you.

"He was guilty of no sin . . . He personally bore *your* sins in His own body . . . By His wounds, *you* have been healed. Why? So you might die to sin and live for righteousness!"*

But He'll never force Himself on you. Do you want Him for your Saviour?

The choice, of course, is yours.

*See I Peter 2:22–24.

CHAPTER 4

The Name of the Game Is Choice

II Kings 17:1–18; 18:9–12; Hosea 11:1–8

"Some People Never Learn!"

This is an expression we're fond of using about other people, for of course it's always the other chap who never learns; naturally it can't be *us*. We go brightly on our way, making all these little "mistakes," for we have all these little quirks to pamper and all these little weaknesses that don't amount to a hill of beans, for they are *ours* and we protect them as though for all the world they were precious and amusing. It's always the *other* chap who is absolutely impossible.

And then when it all catches up with us (and it does) we are shocked and dismayed. "I was only trying to express myself!" we wail. It makes as much sense as playing with a gun and then when it goes off, saying lamely, "I didn't know it was *loaded!*"

The people of Israel were like that. They had their little quirks, like going about their merry way as if God did not exist at all, and all their little weaknesses, like dashing off to worship idols at the drop of an altar. After all, weren't these the characteristics that gave them their personality? And after all, wasn't everybody *else* doing it? So they disobeyed. And disobeyed. And disobeyed. And in their disobedience, they forgot two things.

They were breaking God's heart. And the gun *was* loaded.

They knew it was loaded from the start. Way back when God had delivered them from being slaves in Egypt, and promised them a land which would be their very own. God struck a bargain with them then, and a bargain it was indeed, for they had everything to gain and nothing to lose. "As long as you do right, and obey My laws, you may keep this land; but if you choose to do wrong, you cannot keep it" (see Deuteronomy 30:9,10).

Nothing could be plainer. And it was cheap at the price. They never had it so good.

God Always Does HIS Part

God kept *His* part of the bargain. And He did everything in His power to help them keep *their* part. He put up signposts, road maps, warnings—all the road signs were there. And they weren't left alone to figure out the signs, either. He sent them leaders—one after another.

First Moses.

He took them out of their slavery, into the desert. God guided them with a cloud by day and a pillar of fire by night. He provided food. And water. He parted the Red Sea. He gave them the Ten Commandments. He taught them patiently how to worship. He gave them specific directions how to *build* a place of worship—a tent in the wilderness. And what did *they* do? They grumbled and groaned and complained about everything from the menu (manna) to the monotony (it takes a bit of stick-to-itiveness to hang on).

Oh, how they griped!

And griped. And griped.

Then He sent them Joshua, to get them into the Promised Land. Then He sent them leaders *after* they got there. Samuel. Elijah.

Elijah showed them all that Baal had no power, there on Mt. Carmel—the day the fire came, and the rain. Such a spectacular display of God's power should have turned them back to Him for good, but they were weak in the memory department (that ever happen to you?) and strong on having their own way.

Then God sent Elisha. And Jonah (don't judge Jonah too harshly; he did repent and do as he was told).

"You've Come a Long Way"

During Jonah's time, Jeroboam II was ruling. He was a good king, and the people's hearts were turned back to God. The country reached a prosperity and scope it had not enjoyed since David's rule. Everything was going well.

Yes, Israel had come a long way. And its history could be summed up in a few words: Blessing—sin—punishment—repentance—blessing— And from God's standpoint things could be summed up in a few words too: Bless—warn—punish—forgive—bless—warn—

It was a dreary pattern that kept repeating itself.

But Surely by NOW You've Learned Your Lesson

Israel had sinned so many times, the total was staggering. And God had forgiven the people so many times, *that* total was staggering. Now they were prosperous again. Jeroboam II's rule was the greatest they'd had in many years. God's first promise still held true! "As long as you do right, and obey My laws, you may keep this land; but if you choose to do wrong, you cannot keep it." Surely by now they'd learned their lesson. And it seemed for awhile that they had.

And then Jeroboam II died.

Oh, No—Not AGAIN!

Yes, again. As absolutely incredible as it seems, the people ran into mischief as if they'd never been acquainted with its heartbreak. They took their prosperity for granted and they took God's goodness for granted. Idols were *in* again. And God was *out*.

Surely by NOW God Had Had Enough!

It would seem so. But He is a God of such patience, it is hard for our minds to get hold of it. He gave them yet *again* another chance.

He sent them another prophet. The prophet's name was Hosea, and though the people didn't know it, Hosea was their last chance. They had gone way past the ending; they were living on borrowed time.

"The Love of God Is Greater Far than Tongue or Pen Can Ever Tell"*

God's last message to the people of Israel was one of love. Through Hosea, He told them that He longed to bless them

*From the song "The Love of God."

34

but they would not listen. That He longed to love them but they would not let Him. He told them that He loved Israel as a father loves his young son, and Israel ignored Him and turned to idols. And that He had helped them when they were forming their nation, as a father holds his young son by the arms as he takes his first steps. And they did not even *know* He had helped them.

Then He told them that destruction had to come, for they were determined to disobey Him. And that He had held off His judgment, asking them again and *again* to come back to Him. Why? Because He loved them is why, and it broke His heart to see them come to destruction.

You can read the whole heartbreaking story in Hosea 11:1-4,7,8, "Amplified Bible."

Don't You Know
a "Last Chance" When You See It?

As sad as it was, and as *stupid* as it seems, the people of Israel did not. The fifteen years that followed Jeroboam II's rule? Chaos! The throne changed hands SIX TIMES! Kings were killed wholesale, and their killers ruled in their stead. And then Hoshea came into power.

"The Little Man Who Wasn't There"

Ever hear of the chap who opened the door and nobody came in? Well Hoshea was one of those. *He did that which was evil in the sight of the LORD, but not as the kings of Israel that were before him* (II Kings 17:2).

Here he was, in a crucial time of history, with this great opportunity to lead his people back to God—and he was neither hot nor cold—he was just wishy-washy. He opened the door and nobody came in. He was indifferent to the

35

pleas of Hosea. And the people of Israel were indifferent along with him.

The Beginning of the End

Well Israel had said no to God for the last time. After all, Hosea lived 1,300 years after God's promise to Abraham. 1,300 years is a long time to be patient. And God had been very patient.

The people of Israel continued to sin. And the saddest verse in this whole tale is II Kings 17:9. The people sinned "secretly." The idea was "anything goes, as long as you don't get caught (sound familiar?)." They thought they were deceiving God. But the gun was loaded. And it was about to explode.

Going, Going—

It did explode, like buckshot, in all directions. It was Assyria, that powerful country to the east that was Israel's undoing. It took advantage of Israel's chaos. If the sad tale were told in headlines, it would have gone: ASSYRIA ATTACKS! And: PROVINCES IN THE EAST INVADED! And: DAMASCUS FALLS! And: REFUGEES FLEE! MANY TAKEN CAPTIVE! And: SHALMANESER, KING OF ASSYRIA, DEMANDS TAXES! and: HOSHEA, KING OF ISRAEL, REFUSES TO PAY TAXES! And some of the sad tale wouldn't have got into the headlines. Hoshea made a secret alliance with Egypt. And the alliance "didn't work out." God was not about to help them this time.

The weary months dragged on. Sargon II succeeded Shalmaneser to the throne of Assyria. The headlines would have gone on: SARGON II HAS KING HOSHEA PUT IN PRISON! And: SARGON II LAYS SIEGE TO SAMARIA!

And: WEARY SAMARIA HOLDING OUT! And then, after
three dreadful years: EXHAUSTED, SAMARIA FALLS!

Then the headlines would have stopped. Samaria was
Israel's capital. Israel was finished. It was all over but the
shouting. And there was nothing to shout about.

—Gone

The rest? Just mopping-up operations. The people of
Israel were taken into Assyria, everywhere, some of them
into upper Mesopotamia and some of them into Media and
other places throughout the Assyrian empire. They were
scattered far and wide, separated thoroughly and for good
—they would never get back together again.

It was the end of Israel. Only Judah was left, in the Promised Land.

37

What's It to You?

Now, from all of this, it would seem that you should obey God because if you don't—POW!

What a dreary business! Do you really believe this? Because, if you do, you didn't get the message. Your Lord and Saviour wants you to be His FRIEND. He said, "You are My friends, if you keep on doing the things which I command you to do" (John 15:14, *Amplified Bible*). What did He mean?

A girl (about your age, and this is a true story) went in to her very wise counselor one day, and she was all in a heap (the girl, not the counselor). "Miss Mears," said the girl, "I just don't seem to have any friends. All the other kids have friends. I KNOW the kind of friends I would like to have, but they just don't like me."

"Well now," said Miss Mears, "I have some work to do and it's going to take me about twenty minutes. While you're waiting, why don't you just sit over there—" and she handed the girl a pad and pencil—"and make a list of all the things you would like a friend to be. Then we can talk."

So the girl sat down and began to think. "First I'd like my friend to trust me," she thought. And she wrote down TRUST. "And I'd like my friend to respect me," she thought. And she wrote down RESPECT. Then she chewed her pencil for awhile. "Well I'd sure like to be able to *count* on my friend," she thought, and she stopped chewing her pencil long enough to write down DEPENDABILITY. Then she thought and thought. The most wonderful thing in the world would be to be *understood*. She wrote down UNDERSTANDING.

"What do you have?"

"Hm?"

"What do you have?" It was Miss Mears, finished with her work.

"Oh. Well I wrote down some things—some things, you

38

know, that I'd like a friend to be. But I can't find anybody like that."

Miss Mears read the list. Then she looked up. "Why honey," she said, "that's a *wonderful* list. Just the thing. Now why don't you go out and *be* all of those things—and I'll guarantee you'll find more friends than you can handle!" The girl went on her way, completely mystified at first. Then she thought—did Miss Mears mean that she was to *be* all those things she wanted in a friend before she could *have* friends?

She went home and tacked her list on her closet door and decided to try it. And do you know, while she was working on her list, she picked up so many friends that she didn't know how to handle them all? And she found some very *close* friends too. Ones very special. She understood them. And they understood her. It changed her whole life!

Think on These Things

Think of this girl's list in your relationship with God. Can you trust Him? Respect Him? Count on Him? Understand Him? (You can understand what He is trying to get at in your life by studying His Word.)

Now turn the thing around. Can He understand you? (Read Psalm 139:2, Matthew 9:4 and John 2:24, if you're wondering.) Now. Can He respect you? The very hairs on your head are counted. (Read Matthew 10:30, Luke 12:7.) He respects you as a *person*. NOW. Can He count on you? Trust you? This is up to you. And you can make it true, only with His help.

Oh. One more word. About secret sins. Israel finally fell while she was "secretly sinning." More about secret sins in our next chapter. But meanwhile, make a list of your "secret sins." NOW how do you stack up?

CHAPTER 5

Inside You

II Chronicles, Chapters 29 and 30; II Kings 18:1–16

This is a story you can walk right into. It is extremely personal. It's the story of you.

The cast of characters in this drama is small. Only two. The main character of course is you. The other is your conscience. The conversation between you is very, very private.

As the story opens, you are sitting in your room in your most uncomfortable position. Your face is screwed up and you are pulling on your ear. CONSCIENCE is hovering in the background; you are not aware of him. You are reading. This:

"Everything's in a Mess"

A couple of years before Israel was finally done for, Judah was also having its problems. The people there had

41

turned away from God and were worshiping idols again. Their king was King Ahaz, and a weak one he was. He had spent most of the national treasury and the country was in turmoil. For years enemies had been invading, carrying off both loot and citizens, and taking possession of cities. Once, in desperation, King Ahaz had sent a large treasure to Assyria in return for help. Assyria kept the treasure, yes. Assyria sent help, no. Things went uncomfortably from bad to worse. But the people kept on worshiping idols. And King Ahaz did nothing to stop them.

There was a young man growing up in Judah during these troubled times. His name was Hezekiah. He saw what was going on around him. And he had plenty to worry about. For King Ahaz was *his father*.

Someday he would have to take his father's place. And make decisions. And take responsibility. There were no two ways about it, he had inherited a *mess!* and none of it was his fault.

CONSCIENCE COMES FORWARD AND BEGINS TO SPEAK. YOU ARE NOT SURPRISED TO FIND HIM THERE: YOU HAVE SPOKEN TOGETHER OFTEN.

CONSCIENCE: Have a familiar ring?

YOU: Sure does. It's like today's headlines. Wars. Threats of more wars. Country's in a mess. And I'm practically an adult. Well I'm in the doorway or on the threshold or whatever you call it. And look at the shape things are in!

CONSCIENCE: Grumble, grumble, grumble.

YOU: Well look at the world I'm growing up *into!* Sometimes I think I don't want to have anything to do with it. It's hopeless.

CONSCIENCE: But you have a responsibility.

YOU: Me? *I'm* not a king. I'll never be ruling things.

CONSCIENCE: You are the child of a king. God is your

Father. And you are a leader in your own little domain. You can influence people.

YOU: I can't do anything. The whole world's crazy. What am I supposed to do?

CONSCIENCE: Come *on* now. First you size up the problem. You know that. You can't find the answer until you size up the problem. And the *cause* of the problem. That's half the battle. That's what Hezekiah did. You've quit before you've started. Why don't you read on?

YOU: Okay, okay.

What's Wrong? Why? What to Do?

Hezekiah sized up the problem. It didn't take much doing; it was painfully obvious. Judah was being invaded; the country was in a mess. The cause? Their forefathers had forsaken the Lord; they had closed the Temple in Jerusalem and *put out the lamps that were to burn continuously there* (see II Chronicles 29:6–8). And his own father had worshiped golden calves and Baal images—and taken the vessels from the Temple and rebuilt them to use for idol worship! (See II Chronicles 28:24.)

The solution was plain enough. *Get back to God.*

"Don't Just Stand There—Do Something!"

Hezekiah was not one to just spout ideas; he was a man of action. He called the priests and Levites, and talked with them. He called them "sons" (II Chronicles 29:11). As "sons" they had a responsibility. No fudging. The priests and Levites were responsible for *worship.*

And they listened, impressed.

They sent for the priests and Levites in the surrounding towns, and *they* came flocking into Jerusalem. The project? CLEAN UP THE TEMPLE.

43

"It's a Mess—Where Do I Start?"

The Temple *was* a mess. Dirt and rubbish had been collecting for years. They carted it out and carried it from the city and dumped it in the valley at the bottom of the eastern slope. Everything that had been used for idol worship? They junked it. Out, out, out. The furnishings that King Ahaz had discarded? They repaired them. And cleaned them up. It took sixteen days. But finally the Temple was clean.

· · · · · ·

CONSCIENCE: Are you getting the message?

YOU: Sure. They cleaned out the Temple. That's great.

CONSCIENCE: Well?

YOU: Well what?

CONSCIENCE: Well, don't you know that *you* are the Temple of the Holy Spirit?

YOU: I remember it—yes—but I don't think I understand it.

CONSCIENCE: If you belong to Christ—

YOU: I have accepted Him as my Saviour.

CONSCIENCE: Then *you* are the Temple of God, and the Spirit of God is dwelling in you. Look at I Corinthians 3:16.

YOU: Oh. I never thought of that. You mean I have to clean out—

CONSCIENCE: Yes. And let's get going. Where do you want to start?

YOU: Well, first, I'm cold. I mean I—when I first accepted Christ I was "turned on" and—and then I got "turned off" somehow and I don't know quite how it happened.

CONSCIENCE: Then let's go to the altar first. What's wrong here?

YOU: It doesn't seem the same as it was. I— Well, I giggle sometimes, and I pass notes when the teacher is teaching. I

44

don't listen. It's like the teacher was reading the telephone book. But sometimes I just stare, and I'm thinking of something else.

CONSCIENCE: That's a good start. But it's the problem, it's not the solution. Let's go down this corridor.

YOU: Do we have to?

CONSCIENCE: We have to, if you mean business. What's behind this door?

YOU: Well I—uh—stretch the truth a little and I tell things about people that aren't quite so, or I—uh—repeat things kids said to other kids just to get in good with the other kids and—uh—well criticize kids to other kids—I just—uh —sort of want to make myself look good—you know how it is—

CONSCIENCE: Stretch the truth? Lying. Repeat things? Gossip. Criticism? Humbug! *Whom* do you think you're making look good? Out with it.

YOU: I won't be popular.

CONSCIENCE: OUT with it. What's behind this door?

YOU: Some ideas I've been playing with. I haven't done them yet. Smoking, for one.

CONSCIENCE: You haven't done it?

YOU: Well, a coupla times. It made me feel dizzy. It tasted lousy.

CONSCIENCE: And of course you know that anything that makes you feel dizzy and feel lousy is poisoning your system—and you've heard the medical reports. Out with it. What's behind the next door?

YOU: My thoughts. My secret ones. Do we have to open this one? I'd just as soon skip it.

CONSCIENCE: We have to open this one.

YOU: Picky, picky. picky.

CONSCIENCE: Are you going to clean out the Temple or aren't you?

YOU: I'd rather keep them to myself. They're pretty awful. Sometimes. Sometimes I hate everybody. And sometimes I think—I think—do we have to go into all this?
CONSCIENCE: We have to—
YOU: Why do you keep bugging me? Other kids I know in school do things and their consciences don't bug *them*.
CONSCIENCE: I am a very special conscience. From the moment you accepted Christ as your Saviour, I have been enlightened by the Holy Spirit of God. And I'm going to bug you until you are what He wants you to be.
YOU: Good grief.
CONSCIENCE: What's in here?
YOU: Attitudes. They're—uh—not what they used to be. But it's nothing serious. Just little things. I don't enjoy obeying. I'd like to talk back to my parents. I like to argue. I think most grown-ups are squares. What difference does it make how I *feel*? As long as I go through the motions?
CONSCIENCE: It makes a difference to God. Drag them out and get them repaired.
YOU: Okay, okay. But all this isn't going to be done overnight, you know, so don't hold your breath.
CONSCIENCE: Read on.

. . . . . .

The Temple Is Clean—What Now?

Hezekiah called the priests and Levites to come to a worship service. Then he commanded them to make a sin offering for Judah. Then he ordered music! Lyres, harps, cymbals, tambourines, castinets. The Temple resounded with rejoicing!

But Hezekiah had hardly started. He invited the people to bring sin and thank offerings. And the response was overwhelming. The people poured in in such numbers, the priests had to call for help to take care of the offerings.

Why Not Go All the Way?

Hezekiah was so encouraged, he decided to keep the Feast of the Passover that year. But all this was too much to keep to themselves. Why not invite Israel? Poor Israel, coming apart at the seams, turned away from God. Why not?

So Hezekiah prepared letters and had them sent by runners to the cities in Israel that had not yet been captured by Assyria. "Turn back to the Lord!" the letters said. "Don't be stubborn! The Lord is merciful; He won't turn His face from you if you return to Him!"*

You Can't Win 'Em All

The Israelites laughed at the message and heckled the messengers. *But a few of them came.* They came in such a hurry that they had not had time to perform the ritual required by Jewish law. But Hezekiah told them to join in the feast anyhow. For their *hearts* were right.†

. . . . . .

CONSCIENCE: That ring a bell?
YOU: Sure. After the Temple was cleaned up Hezekiah invited the people to come and make sin offerings.
CONSCIENCE: But you don't have to make a sin offering. Christ was your sin offering on the cross.
YOU: I know that. And I'm grateful. But they had to make sin offerings. And after that, there was music. That means joy. And thanksgiving. But you're talking about witnessing. Inviting other people to turn to God. And a lot of them turn you down. But a few of them come. Okay, okay, I

*Read II Chronicles 30:6–9.

†II Chronicles 30:18, 19.

47

shouldn't be so negative about witnessing. That's one of my attitudes. I know, I know; I'm getting it repaired.

CONSCIENCE: You're getting warm. Think on. What about the ones who came? They were not "ritually clean"* according to law. But Hezekiah welcomed them anyway; their hearts were right. What about the kids who showed up in Sunday School coupla weeks ago. How did you treat them?

YOU: They were oddballs. They looked sort of crumby.

CONSCIENCE: They didn't have *your* little list of do's and don'ts. That it? They were outsiders.

YOU: They had gummy hair. They looked like freaks.

CONSCIENCE: But they were looking for something real. Did they find it in you?

YOU: Now you're making *me* feel crumby. Stop it, will you?

CONSCIENCE: Ouch?

YOU: Okay, ouch. I'm sorry. I really am.

CONSCIENCE: Read on.

YOU: There's more? I don't think I can stand it.

. . . . . .

Put Your Money Where Your Mouth Is

Praise and thanks? Yes. But more was needed. And Hezekiah knew it. God wanted the people to provide for the priests and Levites so they could spend all their time in His service. He put it to them straight. One tenth of their harvests. And no fudging.

And did they respond! They responded with such enthusiasm that the need was filled and the surplus was piled all over the place until it overflowed onto the Temple court! Every need was met and there was plenty left over!

*They were not practicing the laws of Moses.

. . . . .

CONSCIENCE: Well?

YOU: Now you've hit me where it hurts. How can you do this to me? My allowance is small enough. Good grief.

CONSCIENCE: Well think about it. You decided to clean up your Temple, all the way. Are you willing to go the rest, all the way?

YOU: Yes. But I've got one more question. I'm not going to give in so easily. Judah still had its ups and downs. Those people didn't have it so easy, even after they turned back to the Lord. They were threatened with destruction, you know.

CONSCIENCE: Oh, come on now. Haven't you ever read James 1:2—4? Where it says that your trials are to make you strong?

YOU: Yaaaaack.

CONSCIENCE: Now think a minute. You don't get your *physical* muscles lying around in a hammock. You get up and exercise. You should be just as eager to exercise your spiritual muscles. Trials don't separate you from God. Ever read James 1:13, 14? Your own evil desires do, that's what.

YOU: Is that what was wrong with Israel? And the people of Judah, before Hezekiah set them straight?

CONSCIENCE: Of course. And that's what's wrong with you. D'you see?

YOU: Okay, okay. I see. What do I do?

CONSCIENCE: You confess your sins to your Lord as they happen. It's as simple as that.

YOU: Okay. But do you know what? You bug me. But stick around. I might quibble with you sometimes. But I think you are going to do me some good.

CONSCIENCE: You might remember Psalm 86:5: *For thou, Lord, art good, and ready to forgive; and plenteous in mercy unto all them that call upon thee.*

YOU: Okay. Hey, d'you know, I *did* walk right into that story? It's ME.

49

CHAPTER 6

God
Is for Real

II Kings 18:13–19; II Chronicles, Chapter 32; Isaiah, Chapters 36 and 37

"I'm Behaving Myself,
But the Problems Are Still There"

Oh, come on now. You wouldn't want to be like a puppet, would you, going through motions as if someone was pulling your strings. And without any battles to fight?

Hezekiah was behaving himself too. But problems! They were gigantic! Assyria finished devouring the northern kingdom of Israel and then swooped down into Judah "like a wolf on the fold," as the poet puts it. City after city was taken, until only Jerusalem was left.

Hezekiah didn't hang around and wait for anybody to pull his strings. He waded into his problems with gusto. He ordered the manufacture of more shields and weapons. He gathered his army. With feverish haste he had the walls of Jerusalem repaired and fortified, waiting for the onslaught. He looked beyond those walls to the Gihon Spring that supplied the city with water. "Why should our enemies find water?" he thought. So he gathered skilled workmen and they dug a great conduit—an emergency tunnel—to bring the water into the city. They brought that water 1,750 feet through solid rock, into the pool of Siloam within the city walls, and covered the outer entrance to the spring so their enemies wouldn't find it. They bored from both ends—in feverish haste—until the day when there were only five feet more to be bored through, and the workmen called back and forth to each other, through a crevice in the rock. And they struck, drill upon drill, to meet each other. And finally the last bit of rock came crashing down and the water flowed through. And they cut the record of it in the rock on the tunnel walls. Talk about facing problems!

"How Long Do I Have to Hang On?"

You might *ask* this question, but while you're asking it— *don't let go.* Just keep on "hanging on!"

Hezekiah went to Sennacherib,* stationed in Philistia. He humbled himself and said, "Let us come to some agreement; I will pay you tribute—whatever you ask." Sennacherib's answer was a stunning blow. He asked for such tremendous sums of gold and silver that Hezekiah could not pay it without robbing the Temple of its treasures. And he used up the treasures of his own house. And it *still* wasn't enough. He

*The Assyrian ruler.

had to strip the gold from the pillars and doors of the Temple itself.

"But Can't I Depend on People?"

Depends on whom you depend on. Hezekiah flirted with the idea of depending on Egypt. But Sennacherib began to smack *his* lips over Egypt. The wicked So, pharaoh of Egypt was dead, and his nephew Tirhakah was reigning. (So's son would have been reigning, only he'd been murdered by Tirhakah. So you can see who poor Hezekiah was flirting with. Real nice people.) *Anyhow,* Tirhakah rashly matched strength with Sennacherib, and invited Hezekiah to join him. "You will be a strategic enemy," he said. "You will threaten Sennacherib's door."*

Here's where Hezekiah gets even? No, here's where Hezekiah gets into trouble. He defied Sennacherib and all the Assyrian hordes, and announced Judah's independence. Sennacherib and Tirhakah clashed. Egypt was pulverized. Which left Sennacherib the unchallenged conqueror of the day. It was as if great big Assyria was now looking over at tiny Judah and roaring, "And now—what were you saying?"

"But Things Are Getting Worse and Worse"

Sure. Sometimes they get worse before they get better. Hang on. Let's see what happened.

You can imagine the position of Hezekiah. He was left defending Jerusalem and defying the greatest military power in the world. Sennacherib had brushed Egypt off like

---

*You're confused! Don't worry about it—so were they. They never did get it straight.

53

a fly off his beard. And while he was busy mopping up, he sent his general Rab-shakeh and two other high officials to lay siege to Jerusalem and demand Hezekiah's surrender. The people inside the city walls were terrified. There came the Assyrians with their archers, their horses, their chariots, their siege engines—all of it. The works.

And there stood Sennacherib's general Rab-shakeh, proud, scornful. And he cried over the city wall to the people of Jerusalem. "Thus saith the GREAT king, the king of Assyria, 'You say you have strength for war against ME? Where is your strength? In whom are you trusting? In Egypt? Ho! Egypt is like a bruised reed. If a man should lean on it, it would go into his hand and pierce him. So Hezekiah made you defy ME?* Does he not persuade you to bring death upon yourselves with starvation and thirst, telling you that God will deliver you from the Assyrians?' "

Good grief, Rab-shakeh was speaking in Hebrew. And the people who had gathered on the city wall could understand every word he said. The spokesmen of Hezekiah were frantic. Why panic the people? They shouted back, "Speak we pray thee in the Syrian language. We can understand you—speak not in the language of all these people who can hear you—"

"Ha!" Rab-shakeh boiled over. "Hath my master sent me just to you? Hath he not sent me to these people also? Hear me, people—let not Hezekiah deceive you. Don't let him make you trust in God for deliverance. He will not be able to deliver you from the hand of Sennacherib! Have any gods of any OTHER nations delivered THEM out of his hand? Where are the gods of Hamath, of Arpad? Have they delivered Samaria? Well? Name all the gods of all the countries! Name one god who has delivered his people from Sennacherib. What makes you think that Jehovah will deliver Jerusalem?"

*Sennacherib, that is.

54

No answer. Hezekiah's commandment had been "Answer him not."

Well they didn't answer. But the problem wasn't solved. There was trouble abrewing, trouble aplenty. Things were never worse.

"If All Else Fails—Call on God"

Well it sounds like a snitty thing to say. But it is what we *do*, sometimes. (Even us nice Christians!) It is what Hezekiah finally did. He'd tried everything else first.

Eliakim, who was the overseer of the palace, and Shebna, a scribe, and Joah, a trusted servant, all went to Hezekiah and told him all that Rab-shakeh had said. And Hezekiah was scared. He sent them to the prophet Isaiah right off. And Hezekiah went to the Temple to pray.

It was about time.

Right about now, you're thinking, Hezekiah depended on Isaiah. *He was people. So why can't I depend on people?* Think again. It depends on *which* people you're depending on. Isaiah was a prophet of God. Hezekiah had smartened up at last.

Hezekiah's message to Isaiah was: "This is a day of extreme danger. Pray for the people of Judah."

But in the Temple, Hezekiah thought: "Blasphemy! That's what it was. Sennacherib had insulted the living God of Israel!" Even in the middle of his fright, he thought: "How DARED Sennacherib do such a thing? Was God going to stand for THIS?"

And before Hezekiah had hardly prayed his prayer, the answer from Isaiah came back: "Thus saith the Lord: Be not afraid of the words that thou hast heard, wherewith the servants of the king of Assyria have blasphemed me. Behold, I will send a blast upon him, and he shall hear a rumor, and

55

return to his own land; and I will cause him to fall by the sword in his own land."

Wow.

"I Thought My Problem Was Solved. What's This?"

Oh, come *on* now. Every problem isn't solved, all tied up in a neat little package. There might be complications. It's what makes life interesting. Read on.

Rab-shakeh went back to his master and told him he could get no answer from those stubborn Jews, though he'd shouted his head off over the city wall. They just didn't scare. So Sennacherib wrote Hezekiah a letter. A very insulting letter: "Let not your God in whom you trust, deceive you—telling you I won't conquer Jerusalem. You have unquestionably heard what the kings of Assyria have done to all the lands in completely destroying them, and shall you be delivered? Did the gods of the other nations deliver them?" And so forth. Much the same as Rab-shakeh had shouted over the city wall.

"But Sometimes God Seems So Far Away"

Yes. Sometimes He does. And you feel like a blob. And He seems to be just an *idea*—not a real person at all. You lose touch. And get scared.

Hezekiah was at the end of his rope. And he COULD have considered God an abstract thing. Not caring. Not knowing. Nothing was for real. And surely, right now, God was not for real. Everything was going from bad to worse. Hezekiah COULD have put the letter away in his files and given up. God was far away; the letter was a very real thing, right there.

But for Hezekiah, God was *very real*. Hezekiah *spread that letter out before the Lord*. Just as if the Lord were looking over his shoulder. *That's* how real God was.

"God Is for Real?"

Well Hezekiah thought so. He spread that letter out, and he cried: "Oh, Lord, God of Israel, God of all the earth, Thou hast made the heavens and the earth. Listen, Lord— look and see what Sennacherib hast sent to insult Thee. It is true, what he says. The kings of Assyria HAVE laid waste the nations and their lands, and have given their gods to the flames, but they were no gods. They were THINGS— IDOLS—made with men's hands—so the enemy could destroy them. But Thou, Thou art NOT an idol. Thou art GOD. Deliver us, we pray Thee, that they may know that Thou art God—"*

That's some prayer. Makes you shiver.

*See II Kings 19:15–19.

"And God Will Deliver Me from My Problems?"

Well, Hezekiah had no sooner spread his letter before the Lord than a message came back from Isaiah: Jerusalem would NOT be destroyed.

And how did God accomplish this? Remember Isaiah's prophecy? "Behold, I will send a blast upon him, and he shall hear a rumor, and return to his own land; and I will cause him to fall by the sword in his own land."

It all came true. Like a landslide. All at once. The rumor? That the king of Ethiopia was marching against Sennacherib's own country. It made Sennacherib jump out of his skin. And decide to get his army back home, and quick. The blast? That very night, the angel of the Lord went into the Assyrian camp and killed 185,000 of his warriors! The Bible tells us that "Sennacherib, king of Assyria, departed." The literal translation, more accurately, would be "So Sennacherib, king of Assyria, 'beat it.'" That he did. Imagine awakening in the morning to find most of your army gone—killed mysteriously!

He "beat it" for two reasons. One, to defend his own country, and two, because he was scared to death! As the poet puts it—"The Assyrian came down like a wolf on the fold, and his cohorts were gleaming in purple and gold—" And the end: "And the might of the Gentiles,° unsmote by the sword, hath melted like snow† at the glance of the Lord."

"Will the Problem Come Back?"

Your problems might. But this problem didn't. Sennacherib never got around to coming back. And the rest of

°Sennacherib's army.

†And it sure **did**. Melt, that is.

Isaiah's prophecy? Few years later, Sennacherib was murdered by his own sons. And that was the end of Sennacherib—mighty Sennacherib—but he couldn't conquer little Judah.

He hated to admit that. He even fixed his records up to make his defeat look like a victory—to save face. He couldn't say he conquered Jerusalem—he never even got INSIDE it. So Sennacherib carved on his records—they're on a big clay prism in the British Museum today—he carved: "I shut up Hezekiah like a bird in a cage in Jerusalem—I kept him from coming out." That, and a lot more. He even listed tribute Hezekiah paid him, right after that account, to make it look like a victory—but the list of tribute was the same one Hezekiah had paid a long time before, when Sennacherib had first threatened him. By repeating it there, he hoped to fool posterity. But the Word of God is unshakable.

Sennacherib's army was really greater than Hezekiah's. But Hezekiah had put his trust in God. And when you do that, there's only one kind of strong you need to be. "Strong in the LORD, and in the power of HIS might."

CHAPTER 7

Lost
Treasure Found!

II Chronicles, Chapters 34 and 35; II Kings, Chapters 22 and 23

Hilkiah was prowling through the Temple. The dust was heavy in the air; you could almost taste it. And the noise! Everywhere he looked, workmen were busy, grunting, straining, shouting orders, as incredibly huge stones were being hoisted up by ropes into place, to fill gaping wounds in the walls. The sun shone through the holes and sent shafts of light, filled with dust, to the floors. And the floors! Rubble everywhere. Three generations of it. Piled, strewn, kicked aside—three generations of neglect.

It was seventy-five years since the good king Hezekiah had ruled, when the Temple had been in its glory, and the people had been glad and prosperous before the Lord.

75 years! In 75 years, two bad kings had reduced the

country to ruin. Hezekiah's son. And his grandson. And the Temple was in shambles.

But Hilkiah was a happy man. He was a high priest there in the Temple in Jerusalem. And at last a good king had come along again. Hezekiah's *great* grandson. The good king Josiah. The country was back in shape again. And the Temple was being repaired!

Hilkiah had orders to take the money that came in the Temple treasury and hire workmen to clean up, to fix up, and to get back to business for the Lord again!

He prowled on, poking into chambers, pushing aside rubbish, backing away from the clouds of dust every movement sent up—

What was this?

He stepped back from a pile of junk that came down like a landslide. And rummaged with his foot. It was a scroll. He stooped, picked it up. And examined it. Carefully. It couldn't be. But it *had* to be.

He took it up carefully, put it under his arm, and hurried out of the Temple and to the palace. He had just discovered something that had been lost for three generations!

. . . . . .

In the palace, Shaphan was poring over his account books. He was the good king Josiah's chief scribe, and the overseer of the repairs of the Temple. And he, too, was a happy man. Things were going great. King Josiah had been a good king, from the beginning of his reign. He had swept out, like a new broom, all the rubbish that had accumulated since Hezekiah's good rule. Destroyed idols, put the people back on their feet. And now he was repairing the Temple.

Shaphan rummaged through his papers. There was still much work to be done. More stones to be cut. And hauled. More timber to be cut.

"Sire?"

It was a servant.

"Yes?"

"The high priest, Hilkiah, wishes to see you."

"Tell him to come in."

Shaphan was prepared for a further report on the work. He was totally unprepared for what Hilkiah pulled from under his arm.

The dust still clung to it, as Shaphan took it—and began to unroll it. And then he began to read. Hilkiah stood silently as Shaphan read on for a few moments. Then they stared at each other.

"Where did you find this?" Shaphan asked.

"In the Temple."

"It is the Book of the Law."

"I know."

"It tells good news—and bad news."

"I know."

"I must show it to the king."

"I know."

. . . . . .

In his private quarters, King Josiah stared out the window in the direction of the Temple. It was hard for him to remember when he hadn't been king. For he'd been crowned when he was only eight years old.

Others had ruled for him at first, but by the time he was sixteen he'd begun to make his own decisions. He'd decided to follow the Lord. His grandfather had turned Judah to idol worship. His own father had followed the same course. And had been murdered by his own palace slaves. He'd be different, Josiah had decided. And he had been.

By the time he was twenty, he'd organized the biggest cleanup campaign in the history of Judah. Idols? Out! Altars? Down! And the job was thorough. Pillars burned. Metals melted. Stone crushed to powder and sprinkled on the graves of all the dead priests who'd been idol worshipers. And Josiah had traveled all over the country to see that it was done.

And now, at twenty-six, he was repairing the Temple. It was a good life. And he had a great God.

Josiah was counting his blessings when the knock came at his door. It was a servant. Shaphan the scribe desired an audience with the king. The matter was very urgent.

. . . . . .

Shaphan came into the room as if he couldn't believe what he was about to say.

"Hilkiah the priest gave me this book," he said, and handed the scroll to the king. It was incredible. The very Word of God! Lost for a hundred years, lying under the rubble in the Temple! And no one had known it was there, had even missed it.

The king examined the scroll in wonder. Then he handed the scroll back to Shaphan, and sat down, shaken. "Read it to me," he said.

Shaphan read and Josiah listened. Shaphan read of the promise of blessings if the people obeyed. The promise of punishment if they turned away from God. Words like: *Therefore thou shalt keep the commandments of the LORD thy God, to walk in his ways. . . . And it shall be, if thou do at all forget the LORD thy God, and walk after other gods . . . and worship them . . . ye shall surely perish. As the nations which the LORD destroyeth before your face, so shall ye perish; because ye would not be obedient unto the voice of the LORD your God.* *

In all his life, Josiah had never heard these words read right out of the very Word of God!

Josiah thought of his forefathers who had turned away

*Deuteronomy 8:6, 19, 20.

64

from God. He thought of his own grandfather. His own father. And he tore his clothing in a gesture of grief and mourning.

"Send for the high priest Hilkiah," he said at last. "Our forefathers have not kept the word of the Lord. I have to know what these words mean for us."

.　.　.　.　.　.

Across town, in another part of Jerusalem, Huldah the prophetess sat in her home and listened intently as the VIPs* told her their mission. There was Hilkiah the high priest and some of King Josiah's officials. They had been sent by the king himself. They told her about finding the scroll, and told her of the frightening words they had read in it. Was there any word from the Lord concerning this matter?

They waited in silence for a moment. And then she began to speak. The news was good for the present—and very sad for the future. "Thus says the Lord, the God of Israel, 'Tell the man who sent you to me,'" she began . . .

They listened intently as she went on. The Lord would bring evil upon Judah, because Judah had forsaken Him. But because Josiah's heart was tender, and because he humbled himself before God, his eyes would not see the destruction. He would go to his grave in peace.†

The VIPs hurried out into the streets and back toward the palace.

.　.　.　.　:　.

Back in the palace, King Josiah listened as his VIPs reported what the prophetess Huldah had said. Then he stood, began to issue orders so fast people got stuck in door-

*Very important persons.

†Read II Chronicles 34:23–28.

ways carrying them out. He had heard the Word of God. And he was a man of action. There was more to be done.

. . . . . .

The Temple courts were crammed with people. All the priests, the Levites, the elders from all over Judah were there. And people from the great to the not-so-great, to the least important. From the mighty to the common people. All of them. By order of King Josiah. They had gathered to share in the good news. The Word of God had been found!

And while the people listened silently, the king himself read them the Word of God. And oh, he must have read it with a tender heart. And they must have listened in awe. For when he had finished, he made a covenant with the Lord, before them all. And promised to keep His commandments and do all the things that were written in the book he had read. And the people joined him in that promise, all of them, with great joy.

. . . . . .

The country of Judah was humming with a new excitement. The idols that hadn't been smashed before were finished off. And by order of the king, the Feast of the Passover was celebrated again! It was the first time since King Hezekiah had celebrated it a hundred years before! These were golden days.

And the golden days went on and on and on. For all during the reign of King Josiah, the people of Judah followed the Lord.

. . . . . .

A Bout with Your Conscience

CONSCIENCE: You read the story. What do you think?
YOU: Well first I'm thinking, why did King Josiah turn out to be so good? I mean his father was a louse.

CONSCIENCE: That's one way of putting it.

YOU: Well he was a "bad guy," you know? And his father before him. I mean they were *terrible*.

CONSCIENCE: Everybody has to make his own decisions. Has nothing to do with parents, one way or the other. Everyone is responsible to God for *himself*.

YOU: Whether his parents are good or bad?

CONSCIENCE: Whether his parents are good or bad.

YOU: The other thing is, the Word of God was found. This is very important. I mean they hadn't had it in a hundred years. It was *lost*.

CONSCIENCE: Is *your* Bible lost?

YOU: Well, no. It's right here on my bookshelves.

CONSCIENCE: Do you know what the definition of "lost" is? Look it up, why don't you?

YOU: Okay, okay. (YOU RUMMAGE IN THE DICTIONARY.) Well I know what "lost" is. But it also means "not made use of." And "no longer known." Good grief.

CONSCIENCE: Are you reading it? If you're not, it's lost. Think about it.

YOU: I *do* read it, every once in awhile.

CONSCIENCE: What's the rubble it's under?

YOU: Sorry you asked that. All the rubble of what we talked about the last time, of course. But I'm busy on good things too. School activities and—even church activities— all that stuff. I don't have time.

CONSCIENCE: What happens when you *do* read it? Do you do what it says?

YOU: Sorry you asked that.

CONSCIENCE: Remember James 1:22? *Be ye doers of the word, and not hearers only.* What good does it do if you read it and don't do what it says?

YOU: You are bothering me again. Okay, so I don't always do what it says.

CONSCIENCE: And what about James 1:22–25? The man

who doesn't obey is like a man who looks at himself in the mirror but then goes off and promptly forgets what he is like. So look in the mirror. Your face is dirty. Are you going to go off and leave it that way?

YOU: Yaaack. Okay, *okay.* I get your point.

CONSCIENCE: When the Word of God got to King Josiah, from under the rubble, did he put it in a glass case?

YOU: No, he read it. And did what it said. Not like my Bible on my bookshelves, just lying there. I know, I know. You're getting to me.

CONSCIENCE: Well while I'm getting to you, look up Exodus 24:3,4—the Bible shows you God's laws. And look up John 5:24,39; Acts 18:28—it tells of Christ. And II Timothy 3:15; John 20:31—it tells of the salvation you have through Christ. And I Peter 2:2—it helps you grow in grace. And Psalm 119:105—it is a guide for your Christian living.

YOU: That's a lot of research. Take it easy.

CONSCIENCE: All right, I'll take it easy. But Ephesians 4:25-32 says—Don't hold a grudge; tell the truth; if you steal, you must stop. Do your own work honestly; don't use bad language; stop being mean, bad tempered or angry; be kind to others. And Ephesians 6:1—Obey and honor your parents; work hard all the time—not just when you are being watched. And Philippians 2:4—Think of others— don't be selfish. And Philippians 2:14—Do your work without complaining.

YOU: Stop, *stop!*

CONSCIENCE: Okay, I'll stop. I've given you a rough time. But—

YOU: Yeah?

CONSCIENCE: Don't look now, but your face is dirty.

YOU: I know it is. Boy, is it *dirty!*

CONSCIENCE: Well, think it over.

YOU: Y'know? I don't know why I like you. But I do, in an odd sort of a way.

CHAPTER 8

It Won't
Go Away

II Chronicles 35:20–27; Jeremiah 1:1–10 and Chapter 36

"Don't Upset Me; I've Got My Plans Made"

This is one of the games we play with God, and we get very good at it, for we start to learn it while we're very young. Another name for it is "I've Got My Mind Made Up; Don't Confuse Me with Facts."

"Who *me?*" you say. Well think about it. Have you ever sung "I'll Go Where You Want Me to Go, Dear Lord"—and you're thinking it means somewhere off to distant shores many years from now? And then you're called upon to volunteer to fill some post in your group that'll mean you'll have to stand up and be counted. And you realize it means right now. And you stare at your feet?

In the sleepy little village of Anathoth, two or three miles from Jerusalem, lived a young man. His father was Hilkiah, a priest (not the Hilkiah who found the lost scroll in the Temple). And this young man planned to be a priest too, right there in his hometown where he wouldn't get into any trouble. And he would have lived and died there and never been heard of again except that one day God stopped him in his tracks and sent him spinning. God called him to be a prophet.

"But I Always Bungle Everything"

"I don't know what to say. I fall over my feet. Call on someone else. I'll do it some other time." Is that why you stared at your feet?

Well this young man stared at his feet too. "I am a child," he said, "I'm too young." Now actually he was twenty-one years old. What he meant was, he was afraid of people's scorn, he was afraid he would bungle. But God's answer stopped this young man cold. "Before you were born, I had already chosen you to be a prophet," God told him. "And I'll tell you what to say."

Well!

The task would not be an easy one. He was to warn the people to turn back to God and tell them what would happen if they did not. Clearly, he was not going to be very popular. But he stopped staring at his feet. And he said yes to God. The young man's name was Jeremiah.

As it turned out, he wasn't popular. But his popular friends are long since forgotten. And he is known as one of the greatest prophets in the Bible.

"This Is Harder than I'd Bargained For"

Is it? Hard to take part in your youth group? Harder still to invite school buddies to Sunday School? Hard to talk about the Lord when nobody wants to hear it?

Jeremiah began to talk about the Lord, right there in his own hometown. And immediately he was the most unpopular chap in it. "Prophesy not in the name of the Lord, that you die not by our hand!" they bellowed. They not only didn't want to hear it; they plotted against his life. His own friends!*

Well his friends might have turned against him but God was still there. The Lord warned him of the plot, and he fled for his life to Jerusalem. Now he was out on his own, his bridges burned. No turning back.

"Things Are Going Well; I Hope It Stays This Way"

Naturally if they are, you do. We all do. Who wants problems?

When Jeremiah got to Jerusalem, the young king Josiah was reigning. And as you remember from the last chapter, these were, for the most part, great and golden years. Idols were being destroyed; the people were turning back to God. And as the years went on, the Temple was restored, the lost scroll was found, the Passover was celebrated. Things had never looked better. It's a mistake, however, to think that everybody had suddenly become perfect; it simply was not so. It wasn't so in Jeremiah's hometown and it wasn't so in Jerusalem. There were still sneaky people afoot and there was still reason to give God's warning. But Jeremiah always had King Josiah to back him up.

Years went by. Josiah expanded his territory way up to the plains of Esdraelon. Judah prospered. But something was going on in the surrounding countries that was about to turn everything topsy-turvy again. Babylon was getting stronger. Assyria was getting weaker. And Necho, the king of Egypt, decided to take advantage of Assyria's weakness and march up there and gobble himself up a bit of territory. Carchemish was the town he had in mind, and he had to tangle with Nebuchadnezzar, crown prince of Babylon, to

*Jeremiah 11:21, "Amplified Bible."

get it. What does this have to do with Judah? Well, Necho had to go up the Palestine coast through, you guessed it, some of Josiah's expanded territory, even up through the plains of Esdraelon.

The Carmel mountain range was up there (it was really only a ridge) and there was a pass through it—the pass of Megiddo. Josiah decided to head Necho off at the pass.

"But My Last Human Prop Has Deserted Me"

Sometimes it just seems that way. And sometimes it really happens. The one person we depended on most is taken from us. It's a lonely business.

Josiah waited for Necho at the pass. Necho sent a messenger ahead to warn the king, *What have I to do with you, you king of Judah? I come not against you this day, but against the house with which I am at war; and God has commanded me to make haste. Refrain from opposing God, Who is with me, lest He destroy you* (II Chronicles 35:21, *Amplified Bible*).

But Josiah wouldn't listen. And the battle began. The arrows hissed through the air. And Josiah slumped in his chariot. It was as simple and as quick as that. And as awful as that. "I am severely wounded," he said to his servants. "Take me away."

They took him back to Jerusalem. And he died. That battle had been the first really foolish decision he'd ever made. And it cost him his life.

But oh how he went down in history. "Before him there was no king like him."* A good king.

Jeremiah gave the lamentation at his funeral. And wept. His main support—the man he most depended on—was dead. Jeremiah was alone.

*See II Kings 23:25.

"But My Circumstances Are Against Me"

Sometimes you're just complaining. But sometimes they really are. Things seem to be going to pot. Those in authority over you aren't up to what you'd hoped. And things are really rough.

Jeremiah found it so. The people chose Jehoahaz, Josiah's second son to rule. After three short months, Necho (who claimed Judah as one of his vassals now) threw him out and put Josiah's other son, Jehoiakim on the throne. And you guessed it. Back to idol worship. Things were never rougher.

"But How Am I to Tell Others About God?"

Jeremiah pled, wept, reminded the people of God's love. And warned them of coming judgment. How? He painted vivid word pictures. The enemy would come like a roaring lion out of a thicket (Jeremiah 4:7). Enemies would sweep over the land with chariots like the whirlwind and with horses which were faster than eagles (Jeremiah 4:13).

He used object lessons. Once he took a clay pot to the Temple courts and in front of the crowd, hurled it to the pavement, smashed it. And told the people that Judah would be smashed; God had said so.

For this the governor put him in stocks by the upper Benjamin Gate at the Temple, for everyone to mock.

Nasty business.

But Jeremiah had only begun. He also used the written word. Yes, God told him the words, and Jeremiah dictated them to Baruch, his scribe. It took them a year to get it finished. And it is the book of Jeremiah we have in our Bibles today!

Now *you* don't have to go around smashing pots. Or painting vivid word pictures. Or writing a book. *You** are the

*II Corinthians 3:2.

object lesson. *You* are a living book, for all men to read! Jeremiah's own *life* was his best object lesson!

When the book was finished, Jeremiah sent Baruch to read it to the people in the Temple. He chose a feast day, when crowds would be there. Jeremiah had to stay in hiding. Naturally. He didn't dare show himself. So Baruch went off to the Temple to read the Word.

SOME Will Listen

On fast day, Jerusalem was jammed with people from all over Judah. The Temple courts were crowded. People were milling about, buying sacrifices, arguing, laughing, gossiping. And huddling together. It was winter. It was cold. Suddenly a voice boomed over the crowd, like the voice of doom. People stopped in their tracks, shushed each other, and began to listen.

It was Baruch, on a balcony in the upper court at the entry of the new gate of the Temple. And reading God's love and God's warnings from the scroll, loud and clear.

One man in the crowd listened awhile, then elbowed his way through the throng, to the palace. He was one of the palace princes* and his name was Micaiah. Once inside the palace, into the scribe's chamber where the princes and scribes gathered, he rounded up the other princes. And told them what he had heard. Surely this was word from the Lord. They were impressed. So impressed, they sent a messenger to Baruch and had him brought to the scribe's chamber to read it again. To them.

What they heard was frightening. The questions flew. Where did Baruch get this scroll? Jeremiah had dictated it to him. Where did Jeremiah get it? The Lord gave the words to him.

This could not be brushed aside. The king had to be told.

*A leader, an exalted person clothed with authority.

"Go and hide," they said to Baruch, "you and Jeremiah, and let no one know where you are."

After Baruch had left, they put the scroll in the chamber of one of the scribes, and hurried off to the king. They were frightened.

But most of the people in the Temple courts outside, went about their business, and soon forgot what they had heard.

"Ignore It; Maybe It'll Go Away"

You can, some things. Small problems. Gossip. Rumors. The blues. But you can't ignore the Word of God, and have it go away.

King Jehoiakim sat in his winter quarters, close to the huge brazier.* The coals in the brazier were glowing red. He had heard the news from the princes and had sent for the scroll. Now the princes were gathered around him and Jehudi, one of the scribes, was unrolling the first few columns of it. The crackling of the coals and the unrolling of the scroll were the only sounds in the room.

"Come close," said the king. "Read it to me."

Jehudi began to read. He read of God's love and of Judah's disobedience—one column, two columns, three columns—

King Jehoiakim reached out and took hold of the end of the scroll that had been read. With a penknife, he cut those columns away. And he dropped them on the brazier and the flames shot into the air for a brief moment and died again. Three of the princes spoke up. "Sire, we pray you, do not do this thing," they said, but Jehoiakim ignored them. "Read on," he said to Jehudi. Jehudi read on—of God's warnings,

*A shallow pan for burning coal. It was used for heat, and for cooking.

75

of Judah's coming destruction if the people did not repent. And Jehoiakim reached out and cut the columns away and dropped them on the brazier and the flames shot up again. No one spoke.

Jehudi kept reading on and Jehoiakim kept cutting the columns away and dropping them on the brazier until the last flame had died down. The Word of the Lord was gone, the ashes scattered over the glowing coals. And the Bible says, "Yet they were not afraid, nor did they rend their garments, neither the king, nor any of his servants who heard all these words."*

*Jeremiah 36:24, "Amplified Bible."

You can ignore God's Word, and sometimes you want to, for it does have a way of hitting sore spots and telling you to change things you don't *want* to change.

(There was a letter in an advice column from someone your age and it said: "My mother won't let me do anything I want to do. All she says is clean up your room, pick up your stuff and obey, obey, obey. What can I do with her? MAD." And the answer was brief and to the point: "Dear MAD: Clean up your room, pick up your stuff and obey, obey, obey.")

"But This Thing Is Impossible"

You've come up against a blank wall? You've done your best and everything's failed? Know what God told Jeremiah and Baruch to do? "Take *another scroll* and write on it all the former words that were in the first scroll, which Jehoiakim the king of Judah has burned."* What? A year's work gone down the drain and they had to do it all over *again?* Yes, a year's work gone down the drain and they had to do it all over again.

And they did.

Nothing was impossible, with God.

And the Word of God? Jehoiakim might have burnt it up—but it wouldn't go away.

"But I'm Just Poor Little ME!"

God's promises are the same for you today as they were for Judah then. And His concern for you is greater than you will ever know. You are a Jeremiah, in your own little world. And remember, he was as scared as you are.

And remember—*nothing* is impossible—with *God.*

*Jeremiah 36:28, "Amplified Bible."

CHAPTER 9

What
Is Freedom?

II Kings 25:1–16; II Chronicles 36:11–21; Jeremiah, Chapters 37
and 38

The Word of the Lord to Jeremiah had been scattered in
ashes over the coals on King Jehoiakim's brazier. But burning it did not make it go away, and now every word of it
was about to come true.

The enemy would come like a roaring lion out of a thicket, Jeremiah had said.* He was talking about mighty Babylon, and Nebuchadnezzar, its king.

Years went by after Jehoiakim burnt the scroll, and all
seemed well. Then the lion stirred in the thicket, growling
and threatening. Nebuchadnezzar demanded tribute from
Judah. Jehoiakim paid it gladly to keep the lion in the thicket at any cost. For three years he paid it. And then, because
the lion seemed quiet, he rebelled and withheld the tribute.
But it didn't work.

*Jeremiah 4:7.

The lion came creeping out and settled outside Jerusalem waiting. Nebuchadnezzar came down from the north with his armies and laid siege to the city. And during this siege, Jehoiakim was killed, whether in fighting or by treachery in his own palace, we do not know. But his body was dragged outside the city and left there, like an animal. Jeremiah had said it would happen. And that his subjects would not lament for him saying, Ah, his majesty! How great his glory! No, he'd be buried with the burial of a donkey, dragged out and cast forth beyond the gates of Jerusalem.* It had been written on one of those columns he tossed on the coals.

. . . . . .

The "lion"† retreated back into the thicket again, but not for long. The rule in Judah fell to Jehoiakim's eighteen year old son, who was as wicked as his father had been. He'd no sooner got on the throne when the lion came back and this time it reached inside and Jerusalem felt its claws. Nebuchadnezzar took the young king captive, along with his mother and his wives and nobles and palace officials. And he took the holy vessels from the Temple and all the treasures from the palace. And 10,000 captives—warriors and men of skill—the cream of Judah!

Jeremiah had predicted that none of Jehoiakim's sons would reign. It was one of those columns Jehoiakim had tossed on the coals.

. . . . . .

Now, having given Jerusalem a taste of its claws, the "lion"** went back to the thicket, but now it was snarling, its fangs bared, and Jerusalem could feel its hot breath. Ne-

*Jeremiah 22:18, 19.

†Babylon, and Nebuchadnezzar.

**Babylon, and Nebuchadnezzar, remember?

buchadnezzar chose the new king. Jehoiakim's brother Zedekiah, and the idea was that he was to toe the mark or else. Meanwhile Jeremiah, the Bible tells us, was "going in and out among the people" repeating his warnings over and over again. The people were indifferent to him. King Zedekiah's officials downright hated him. And Zedekiah himself?

He was another king, who, when he opened the door nobody came in. There were his hostile and godless officials. There was the steadfast Jeremiah. And there were other prophets in town who were braying false hopes that all would be well, Jerusalem would not be destroyed. And Zedekiah fluttered from one to the other like a canary turned loose in the house, not knowing where to go.

Every time things simmered down, he listened to his officials and the false prophets. Every time a crisis came he sent secret messages to Jeremiah, "Is there any word from the Lord?" And every time Jeremiah told him the truth he ignored it.

Once it looked as if the false prophets were right. Egypt actually marched north to help! And when the news came of Egypt's approaching army, Nebuchadnezzar's armies withdrew from Jerusalem and the Bible tells us, "departed."

Good news! The false prophets were right. And what did Jeremiah have to say now?

With all the evidence against him, Jeremiah stuck to his guns. The Egyptians would return to their land, he said. *But Nebuchadnezzar would be back.* "Do not deceive yourselves," Jeremiah warned doggedly, "they will surely be back."

And as he had told them, the Egyptian army *did* go back home. The first part of his prophecy had come true.

BUT.

The stage was set for the final pounce of the "lion."* But

*Babylon, and Nebuchadnezzar, of course.

before it happened, Jeremiah, who had once cried out to the Lord, "I am afraid of their faces!" timid Jeremiah, was in for some of the roughest testing of his life.

. . . . . .

The sentry stood by one of the city gates. There was an uneasy quiet over Jerusalem. People were allowed to come and go, but everyone was suspect. The sentry watched the people come and go, scanning each face, and then—

He leaped forward, grabbing one man and pulling him out of the crowd. It was Jeremiah.

"You are deserting to King Nebuchadnezzar and the Babylonians," he accused.

"That is not true," said Jeremiah, who was only going to Anathoth to get the title to his portion of land among his people.

"I don't believe you," said the sentry, and began to hustle him off.

"Where are you taking me?"

"To the princes."*

This could be nothing but trouble.

. . . . . .

Jeremiah sat in a dungeon cell. The welts on his body were still there, after many days in prison. He had been severely beaten by the king's officials and left there, for all he knew, to rot. The lion had come out of the thicket again while Jeremiah was in the dungeon, and was crouching outside the city walls, waiting, watching.

Well, Jeremiah had fought the good fight. And now it was over. He knew what God had told him to say was true. Jerusalem would fall. He might not live to see it, but it would fall.

*The king's officials.

The door of his dungeon creaked and opened. It was a guard from the palace. He was being sent for secretly by King Zedekiah. But only to be questioned.

. . . . . .

It was quiet in the king's private quarters. The guard had ushered Jeremiah in, closed the door, and was waiting outside. The two men faced each other alone. The king, regally dressed, fearing he might be wrong. Jeremiah, battered, his clothing torn, knowing he was right. The king looked at Jeremiah nervously.

"Is there any word from the Lord?" he said.

Jeremiah looked back, unwavering. He was a prisoner. He could say what the king wanted to hear and be free.

He made his choice.

"There is," he said quietly. "You shall be delivered into the hand of the king of Babylon."

There was silence.

"And where have I sinned against you, or your servants, or these people, that you should put me in prison?" Jeremiah went on.

No answer.

"And where are the prophets now who said the king of Babylon would not come against you?"

No answer. There *was* no answer. Jeremiah followed up his advantage. "Therefore I pray you that you do not let me be returned to the dungeon, lest I die there."

King Zedekiah summoned the guard. "Transfer him to a cell in the court of the guard," he said. "And give him bread to eat."

The interview was over.

. . . . . .

The siege continued. The "lion"* lay crouched outside,

*Babylon, and Nebuchadnezzar, naturally.

83

biding its time; there was no hurry. The days turned to weeks. And the food began to grow scarce.

. . . . . .

King Zedekiah faced his officials, in his private quarters. He was a man trapped. He'd never been true to anything. He'd constantly inquired about word from the Lord, and refused to obey it. He was even at the mercy of his own officials.

"We beseech you, let this prophet of doom be put to death," they told him. "All of his preaching has lowered the morale of the soldiers and the people. He hasn't thought of their welfare; he's meant them harm from the beginning!"

The king held their gaze for a moment, then looked away. "He is in your hands," he said at last. "I am in no position to do anything against you."

. . . . . .

The king's officials and some common soldiers were huddled around a cistern in the court of the guard. The cover had been rolled aside, and they were lowering the man down into the cistern with ropes. There was no water at the bottom, only a slimy mire. The man sank into it; they jerked the ropes loose and rolled the cover back on, and left him there.

The man was Jeremiah.

. . . . . .

The confrontation was a strange one indeed. Two men, facing each other. One was very weak; one was very strong. The weak one was the king. The strong one was an Ethiopian, a black man, a slave in the king's court. His name was Ebedmelech, and he was willing to get involved in someone else's problem, even to the risking of his life.

"My Lord the king, these men have done evil to the prophet Jeremiah. They have put him into the cistern in the court of the guards. He is sunk into the mire at the bottom. And he is as good as dead if we don't get him out."

For once the king made a snap decision, and on his own. "Go," he said. "Take thirty men from here with you. Get him out. Before he dies."

The black man hurried from the room.

. . . . . .

Thirty men and Ebedmelech huddled over the cistern. The ropes had been lowered, with rags and worn-out garments tied to them. Ebedmelech had gathered the rags and garments from the house of the king under the treasury. He was now on his hands and knees, calling down.

"Put the rags and garments under your armpits," he called, "and over the ropes." They waited. At last Jeremiah called back that he was ready. And they began to pull, slowly at first, until he came out of the mire with a great sucking sound, and they drew him carefully up, up, until they dragged him over the side, and he lay on the pavement, exhausted. He had to be returned to a cell in the court of the guard. But he was alive. The only man alive in Jerusalem who was God's spokesman.

. . . . . .

The "lion"* played with its prey as a cat does with a mouse. Retreating, coming back, always coming back. Inside the city there was low morale everywhere, and hopelessness. The farms had been trampled into dust, neglected and barren. There was no food coming in. And the food already there was dwindling at an alarming rate. The rich and poor alike were starving. But no one thought of turning back to God. They still worshiped idols. And mocked Jeremiah.

*Babylon, and Nebuchadnezzar. Who else?

85

Outside the city was always Nebuchadnezzar; he would no sooner go away than he would come back again. And there he'd stay, with his tents and armed men and loads of provisions. No one could go out or come in. The "lion" was always there. Waiting to strike.

. . . . . .

*"I'm going to ask you something. Hide nothing from me." It was King Zedekiah. Talking to Jeremiah, dragged fresh out of prison again.

"If I tell you, you will put me to death," said Jeremiah. "And if I give you counsel, you will not listen to me."

"As the Lord lives, I will not put you to death or give you into the hands of my officials," Zedekiah said quickly.

The two men stared at each other, Jeremiah beseechingly, the king half defiant, half afraid. "Then here is what God has told me," said Jeremiah. "If you give yourself up to Nebuchadnezzar the city shall not be destroyed. And you shall live, you and your family. If you do not, the city shall be destroyed. And you shall not escape, you or your family. Obey, I pray you, the voice of the Lord who speaks to you through me."

Zedekiah hesitated a moment. This was the moment he had to make up his mind. This was his moment of truth. And he blew it.

"Let no one hear of our conversation," he said. "If my officials ask you, tell them nothing. You may go."

Jeremiah left, with his guards, back to prison. And Zedekiah did not know it, but he had blown his last chance, his absolutely last chance, into thin air. He had defied God for the last time.

. . . . . .

*See Jeremiah 38:14–24.

The "lion"* crouched on its haunches, ready for the spring. And with a snarl, leapt through the air toward its prey.

. . . . . .

"Breach in the walls!"

The cry went throughout Jerusalem. One of Nebuchadnezzar's battering rams had sent a section of the wall shivering, buckling, crashing inward, leaving a gaping opening.

This time Nebuchadnezzar had not come just to rob the Temple and take some hostages. This time the "lion" was moving in for the kill. Into the breach the army poured, with stones and slings and arrows and spears and javelins and swords, spilling into the narrow streets, and everywhere there was terror and the din rose to the skies.

And those who could, fled out through what gates they could, even the men of war. And even the officials. And even the king.

Zedekiah got clear to the plains of Jericho before Nebuchadnezzar's soldiers caught up with him.

. . . . . .

Jeremiah was in his cell in the court of the guard, listening to the din outside when the enemy soldiers broke in and got him. He was hustled without ceremony through the streets and into a safe area. Nebuchadnezzar had left orders that he was not to be harmed. And he stood there, free at last, watching his beloved Jerusalem burning. The palace, the Temple, the houses, everything burning. And the walls buckling, now in this place, now in that, crashing to the ground. And he wept for his people who had defied God because they'd wanted to be free . . .

. . . . . .

*Babylon and Nebuchadnezzar. You know by now?

Zedekiah stumbled along with thousands of others prisoners, on the long trek to Babylon—along with the loot and the brass pillars and furniture from the Temple. The officials he'd foolishly listened to so often had been killed. And back in Riblah, where the enemy's army supplies were kept, they'd stopped awhile for a trial. And his sons had been killed before his eyes.

But now his eyes were gone, for they had been put out by his tormentors, and he was being led, bound in shackles. And he wept—for he had refused God's love, and now it was too late.

· · · · · ·

Jeremiah walked along the road, weary but unharmed, on his way to the town of Mizpah, outside Jerusalem. He was with Gedaliah, a prominent man in Mizpah. Nebuchadnezzar's officials had entrusted him to Gedaliah's care. The enemy king had given Jeremiah a choice, too—did he want to go to Babylon or stay near Jerusalem with the few who were left behind to farm the land outside the broken down walls? He'd chosen to stay and live out his life and serve his Lord near his beloved Jerusalem.

· · · · · ·

The few who were left behind to farm had escaped with their lives in one way or another.

But there was one among them who was saved by specific order of the Lord. God had told Jeremiah that he would deliver this man, that he would not fall by the sword because he had put his trust in Him. The man was Ebedmelech. The black man, who believed God enough to get involved and risk his life to save Jeremiah.

· · · · · ·

The smouldering fires of Jerusalem could be seen for days, and the smoke rising from the desolation. The holy city was gone. And Judah was finished. The people had wanted to be free; in their self-chosen freedom, they had found only destruction. And in their blindness they had failed to see that their true freedom lay in God . . .

.   .   .   .   .   .

Your own brand of "freedom" may be slavery in disguise. "For a man is a slave to whatever controls him."* Are you a slave to anger? Your emotions? Your desires? Whatever it is, if you're obeying it you're a slave to it. The Christian law is the law of *liberty*. It's only when you accept the will of God and obey the law of God that you are really free—free to be the terrific person you want to be!

"If the Son therefore shall make you free, ye shall be free indeed."†

*II Peter 2:19, "The Living New Testament, Paraphrased." (Wheaton: Tyndale House, Publishers, 1967.) Used by permission.

†John 8:36.

CHAPTER 10

To Do or Not to Do— That's the Question

Daniel, Chapters 1,2 and 3

"When in Rome, Do as the Romans Do"—"or Do You?"

Ever stop to think of what it might be like to go off to a faraway land, get to live in a king's palace and have your heart's desire? Beautiful clothes, the best of food, an expensive education, and the promise of being put in an important position and live in comfort for the rest of your days?

There'd be only one hitch. You'd be expected to go along with the customs of the palace. And this would include doing some things God has expressly forbidden you to do. It would mean turning your back on God. If you went along, everything would be great. If you did not, you faced the possibility of—

POW!

This actually happened to four boys from Jerusalem, during those last terrible war-torn years. They were from families of the nobility but in those days even the noble families did not fare very well. And during one of King Nebuchadnezzar's invasions, these boys were among the captives toted off to Babylon.

"But the Great Big World Is Exciting"

Babylon! The greatest, the most powerful, the most beautiful city in the ancient world! It was like a product of some day dreamer's fanciful imagination. The city wall rose 344 feet in the air, reinforced with imposing towers at intervals. And so thick* was it, the top was made into a highway, with rooms built along the edges. Here was the place to take an afternoon ride and show off your late-model chariot. And no danger of side swiping, either. It was wide enough for four-horse chariots to ride easily, and even pass each other. You could ride along and look out over the surrounding country, or look in toward that marvelous city, over the inner wall. (Yes, there was another wall inside, for extra protection.)

Beyond the inner wall you could view the many temples, the wide beautiful streets and highways, the extensive parks, the fertile fields. You could admire Nebuchadnezzar's palace—a huge complex of magnificent buildings protected by a massive double wall. And you could goggle at the hanging gardens, a profusion of plants and palm trees on terraces† that went up, up, up, to different levels until they

---

*86 feet.

†Supported on huge masonry arches. The hanging gardens were built by Nebuchadnezzar for his queen, who was homesick for her hilly home country of Media.

towered so high they were visible above the tallest buildings. One of the seven wonders of the ancient world!

The Euphrates River ran *under huge gates*, right through the middle of the city, separating it into two halves. Inside the city, the river was walled, like a great canal, and ramps led up from the water to gates that led to the city streets.

There were other gates, too, in the huge outside walls—eight of them, all beautifully decorated with enameled brick. And naturally, heavily guarded.

The city inside being guarded was like a world of its own. This was the world into which these four boys were dumped. And the story would have ended there, except for one thing.

To Do or Not to Do—That's the Question

King Nebuchadnezzar wanted some of the captives from Jerusalem to be trained for important positions in his court. And he wanted the best, from the nobility.

"Pick strong, healthy, good-looking lads," he told his chief marshal, "those who have read widely in many fields, are well informed, alert and sensible, and have enough poise to look good around the palace."* And you guessed it. These four boys were among those chosen. Their names were Daniel, Hananiah, Mishael and Azariah. But the counselor in charge of them promptly changed them. He changed Daniel's name to Belteshazzar (but the name didn't stick; he was always known as Daniel). The names the counselor gave the other three *did* stick, and we know them today as Shadrach, Meshach and Abednego. And so their new life began.

*Daniel 1:4, "Living Prophecies: The Minor Prophets Paraphrased." (Wheaton: Tyndale House, Publishers, 1965.) Used by permission.

A three year training program. Learn the language, learn the culture, train for positions of leadership under the best tutors, live like kings—

There was only one hitch.

They were expected to go along with the customs of the palace.

And that included doing some things God had expressly forbidden them to do. It meant turning their backs on God. If they went along, everything would be great. If they did not, they faced the possibility of—

POW!

"But It's Such a Little Thing"

The first problem didn't seem too serious at first glance. Just eat the special diet sent from the table of the king. "Rich and dainty food," the Bible tells us. Nothing but delicacies! Nothing wrong with that.

Except that it was the custom in that country to consecrate each meal by offering a portion of those "delicacies" to the heathen gods. And some of the meat the Jews had been expressly forbidden to eat.*

Now it would be no easy job to go to the counselor and tell him you couldn't eat that diet because it didn't come up to the standards you'd been brought up on, and couldn't you please have something else, something that met your standards? Phew!

But it's exactly what Daniel did.

"What?" said the counselor. "But you won't be merry, as the others! Your faces will be pale and sad. And the king will have my head!"

"Prove us," said Daniel. "Just give us a vegetable diet and water to drink for ten days—"

*Read Numbers 6:1–4 and I Corinthians 10:21.

94

"Vegetables? *Water?*"

"For just ten days," Daniel persisted, "and compare us with the other youths. And deal with us according to what you see."

Now ordinarily this kind of boldness would have put Daniel in the brig, but God had put a love for Daniel in his counselor's heart. And instead of getting punished, Daniel got his way.

The four lads tackled their vegetable diet with cheerfulness, and at the end of ten days, they were "in the pink." The thing was settled. They stayed on the diet that met their standards.

Seems like a little thing, but it's little things that develop spiritual muscles. God gave them wisdom and understanding and skill. They breezed through their three year training period with no trouble at all, and when they finally stood before the king, they were found to be ten times better than all the learned wise men of that day. And they were put on the king's regular staff of advisors!

But their troubles were not over.

Young Man out on a Limb

Bad news travels fast, and this bad news was buzzing through the palace, leaving all the wise men pale and trembling. It all concerned a dream. If it had been just anybody's dream it would have caused no stir, but this was the king's dream and it was no laughing matter. That it had been a bad dream, the king knew, for it had awakened him in terror. But what it was, he did *not* know, for it had somehow slipped back into his unconscious before he'd hardly pulled the bell cord to summon his servants. His wise men had been called to tell the king what the dream meant, when he didn't know what it *was.*

Now this was pretty unreasonable.

"Tell us what the dream was," they'd pled with him, "and we'll show you the interpretation."

"The thing is gone from me!" he'd bellowed. "*You* tell me what it was!"

"But there is no man on earth who can tell the king what the dream was!" they'd cried.

"No king has ever asked such a thing of any wise man before!"

Well no king ever had before, but King Nebuchadnezzar had done it now. And the bad news was, if *some* wise man couldn't come up with both the dream and its interpretation, *every* wise man in the realm would be killed. When the news reached Daniel, he and his companions were already being sought by the king's executioner.

Daniel decided to be that "one wise man."

Now it was no small matter to go in to the king and make him a promise that was humanly impossible to keep, but Daniel did.

"Give me some time," he said, "and set a date. And I will tell you both the dream and its interpretation."

This was really trusting God.

Daniel went to his three companions, told them the news, "so that they would desire and request mercies of the God of heaven concerning this secret."*

The thing *was* humanly impossible. But now the thing was in God's hands. It's a good place for a problem to be. They prayed. And waited. And prayed. And waited. And then—

"Blessed be the name of God!" cried Daniel. "He reveals the deep and secret things; He knows what is in the darkness! . . . I thank You and praise You, O God . . . Who has given me wisdom . . . and has made known to me now what we desired of You!"†

*Daniel 2:18, "Amplified Bible."
†Daniel 2:20–23, "Amplified Bible."

Sure enough, God had revealed the secret to Daniel. It was time for the action.

. . . . . .

"Are *you* able to tell me my dream and what it means?" the king asked when Daniel was brought before him. It was a catch question, but Daniel came back with the right answer.

"The mysterious secret you demanded to know," he said, "*no man* can show you. BUT. There is a God in heaven who reveals secrets, and *He* has made known to me the interpretation of your dream."

The king leaned forward intently as Daniel began, "You saw a mighty image, dazzling in its brightness, and frightening to look upon. The head was of gold. Its breast and arms of silver. Its belly and thighs of bronze. Its legs of iron.

And its feet part iron and part clay. Then you saw a stone come out of nowhere and crush the image, so that it was pulverized and blew away. And the stone became a great mountain that filled the whole earth.

"That was the dream. Now this is what it means," Daniel went on. "You, O king, are king above all kings on earth. You are the head of gold. The kingdoms that come after you will be strong, but none as great as you are now. But some day the God of heaven will set up a kingdom stronger than any kingdom made by man, and that kingdom will never be destroyed."

The stone that filled the earth, then, was God!

Nebuchadnezzar fell down before Daniel and ordered that incense be offered up in honor of his God. "Your God is the GOD of gods and the LORD of kings and a revealer of secret mysteries!" he cried.

And he gave Daniel gifts and made him chief over all the wise men of Babylon.

And his three friends? At Daniel's request, they were appointed over the affairs of Babylon.

They had arrived.

"It's Harder Here up on Top"

Now a reputation for wisdom is great, and a position of authority is great, but the responsibility that goes along with these things is overwhelming.

As those four lads were placed in higher and higher positions of authority, their tests grew harder. Shadrach, Meshach and Abednego's greatest test came when they refused to bow down to Nebuchadnezzar's golden idol, tall as an eight story building, out on the plain of Dura. They knew they'd be cast into the fiery furnace if they did not bow down. But they did not bow down. And they were.

You know this story well.

"LITTLE Problems
Are to Cut Your Spiritual Teeth On"

But if they'd failed in the first small tests, the chances are slim that they would have passed the big ones when they came. God told one of His prophets once, "If you have raced with men on foot and *they* have tired you out, then how do you expect to compete with *horses?"* *

Another Bout with Your Conscience

YOUR CONSCIENCE: Remember the old song, "Dare to Be a Daniel?"

YOU: Sure. We sing it in VBS and at camp. But I'm no Daniel. Or his friends.

CONSCIENCE: Remember the story of the fiery furnace?

YOU: Oh, sure. They were thrown in, bound in shackles. But the king saw them walking around in there with an angel, and they came out unharmed. Their eyebrows weren't even singed. Cut my teeth on that story. But *I'll* never come up against anything like that.

CONSCIENCE: But their first test was in the king's dining room, over the king's delicacies and the wine. Do you think their decision was right?

YOU: Some kids I know would say they should have gone along with it, you know, maybe just tasted it to be good sports.

CONSCIENCE: What do you think?

YOU: I'll never be in a king's dining room.

CONSCIENCE: But you're in places where people's standards are different from yours. At school. With the neighborhood kids. All sorts of places. So in your own way, you have the same sorts of tests.

*See Jeremiah 12:5.

YOU: Oh, sure. Some of the kids do things I don't do. And the kids in upper grades—well I *hear* things. And sometimes I *think* about those things. But I don't do them. I obey.

CONSCIENCE: *How* do you obey?

YOU: What do you mean?

CONSCIENCE: Daniel and his friends obeyed cheerfully. Their faces weren't sad. At the end of those ten days on their vegetable diet, they were "in the pink."

YOU: Well sometimes when I obey, I *do* feel a bit glum about it all. And sometimes I think I might like to go along with the other kids because I don't want to be chicken.

CONSCIENCE: Daniel and his friends dared to be different. For their Lord's sake. Do you think *they* were chicken?

YOU: They turned out to be pretty strong guys. Where did they get all that strength?

CONSCIENCE: Same place you do. They were empowered by God's Holy Spirit. They depended on God. And God honored them. But at first, their tests were no harder than the ones you face. You race with men on foot first. Then you can compete with horses.

YOU: Hey—is that what that verse means?

CONSCIENCE: What do *you* think it means?

YOU: I'll sleep on it.

CONSCIENCE: While you're sleeping on it, remember that God honors those who follow Him. "If a man wants to enter my service, he must follow my way; and where I am, my servant will also be. And my Father will honor every man who enters my service" (John 12:26, Phillips*).

---

*"The New Testament in Modern English." Copyright J. B. Phillips 1958, twelfth printing 1966. Used by permission of the Macmillan Company, New York, N.Y.

CHAPTER 11

The Party Is Over

Daniel 4:28–37; Chapters 5 and 6

"Proud? Who Me?"

Well think about it. There are all sorts of ways of being proud. Some of us are proud of what we've accomplished. Some of us are proud of what we've got, though we've done nothing to earn it. Some of us are proud of who we are (or think we are). And the rest of us are proud of being humble. It does seem a shame to get everything else in your life nice and tidy, and then get tripped up by your pride.

101

Proud of What You've Done?

Nebuchadnezzar was. He had done a monumental job in building the most beautiful city in the world, and he jolly well knew it. God kept putting him in his place but he never seemed to know enough to stay there. Until one night he was walking on his palace roof looking over the city and he exclaimed "Is not this great Babylon, that *I* have built . . . by the might of *my* power and for the honor and glory of *my* majesty?"*—

And that did it. He'd gone too far.

He'd no sooner made his boast than a voice from heaven said, "O king Nebuchadnezzar, to you it is spoken: The kingdom has departed from you."*

Within the hour he lost his reason and understanding and became desperately ill. And it was seven long years before he came to himself again. But he came back a humble man, recognizing that it was *God* who had given him power. And, to his credit, he honored God till the time of his death.

Proud of Things You Never Earned?

King Belshazzar was. He was three kings later than Nebuchadnezzar.† And a more swaggering, boasting rascal it would be hard to find. He sat in the midst of all this power and splendor, and it never crossed his mind that he'd done nothing to earn it, that he hadn't planned it, that he hadn't built it, that he was indeed ruling it only by the grace of God. And he did not know it, but he was about to get his comeuppance. It was going to come from Cyrus, king of Persia.

. . . . . .

*Read Daniel 4:30,31, "Amplified Bible."

†Probably his grandson, though we don't know for sure.

King of the Mountain?
Watch It—You Could Get Knocked Off

Cyrus was one of the greatest military leaders the world had ever known. He had united the countries of Media and Persia into Medo-Persia and extended his empire to the west until the entire peninsula of Asia Minor was under his rule. By now he was the terror of all Asia. What greater prize could he hope for now than the unattainable Babylon?

And so he marched his armies to Babylon and camped outside that great city. And waited.

. . . . . .

Inside the great city, the people went about their business as usual. They had that strong outer wall—344 feet high and 86 feet thick. And the inner wall—75 feet high and 32 feet thick. And the well-guarded bronze gates. They had plenty of water. They had food enough to last for twenty years. And fields of rich soil, to plant and farm more.

Belshazzar swaggered about his palaces, snug and cozy and proud. Cyrus was camped outside? All right. Let him stay there. Let him stay there till he starved! The city was un-get-inable!

. . . . . .

*Cyrus left most of his army encamped about the city to give the people something to think about, and took the rest of it with him, up, up, along the great Euphrates river bank until they reached what he thought was the likeliest spot. Then they dug in for a stay.

And "dig in" is a good word for it, for "dig" is exactly what he ordered them to do. They gouged a huge excavation out of the earth right next to the river, and left a wall

*From an account by the historian Herodotus.

103

just strong enough to keep the water from running into it.
And then they waited.

The rest of the army down by the city walls was waiting
too. And watching. From a tall tower Cyrus had ordered
them to build they looked over the walls, watching for the
right moment to come.

It finally did. It was on the feast day of the god Bel.

. . . . . .

Inside the city, Belshazzar was giving a great feast to a
thousand of his lords. The banquet hall of the palace was
ablaze with light, the tables were groaning with goodies,
and the servants were filling the wine cups as fast as they
were emptied. And everyone was drinking as if wine was
going out of style. Belshazzar sat, surrounded by his many
wives and his lords, drinking heavily and looking as if he
owned the world. He felt good. So good that he got carried
away.

"Bring in the gold and silver cups King Nebuchadnezzar
got from the Temple in Jerusalem!" he commanded. There
was a hubbub of laughter and talking as they waited for the
cups to be brought in.

"Good," said Belshazzar as they were brought before him.
Those holy cups that had been used for worship in God's
Temple. "Set them down." Those cups that had been han-
dled so carefully by the Temple priests. "Fill them with
wine!" Those cups that had stood where all was quiet and
solemn. "Drink!" He ordered them passed up one table and
down another, to the noisy crowd. And as they drank, they
praised—not God—but their idols of gold and silver and
iron and brass.

They didn't know it, but the party was already over.

Suddenly the king stood up, his face white with terror.
He tried to speak and couldn't—he could only point with
trembling fingers to the wall—and his knees shook so he fell

105

back into his seat again. And as quickly as a crowd can become quiet, that great room was still, everyone looking at that wall.

There was a hand—no arm, no body, just a hand. And the hand was writing. It wrote four words—MENE, MENE, TEKEL, UPHARSIN. And then was gone.

. . . . . .

Outside the city, the orders had been given hours before. A small company of soldiers had gone upstream. And upstream the men had worked feverishly. That retaining wall had been broken down. And the wild waters were rushing over the broken-down bank into new freedom—tumbling, swirling, foaming—down into the huge excavation!

And now, down by the city walls, the tawny waters of the Euphrates began to get lower. Cyrus' generals watched as it went down, down, now with incredible swiftness. Lower and lower. Now under the gates. UNDER THE GATES! Now it was no longer a river. It was now a road: a road that went right underneath the gates and into the city!

. . . . . .

Inside the city, in the great banquet hall of the king, there was a great silence. Everyone was waiting. The hand had disappeared. But the dreadful words had remained. And they were strange words—a language no one had ever seen before. The king had shouted for his magicians and astrologers to be brought before him to tell him what they meant. But they had come and examined the words, and had turned to the king helplessly. No one knew. And now they stood, their mouths gaping open.

It was at this moment that the king's grandmother came into the room. She had heard the excitement. And she had requested an audience with the king. She bowed before him. And everyone waited.

"O king," she said, "do not be alarmed. There is a man in

your kingdom—a forgotten man. And the Spirit of the holy God is in him. And in him is knowledge and understanding and wisdom. He was able to interpret dreams. And clarify riddles. And untie the most intricate knots, in the days of Nebuchadnezzar."

Belshazzar stared at her, his mouth gaping. "Call him," she said. "His name is Daniel."

. . . . . .

Outside the city, orders were given in crisp hushed voices. Every man had his post. Every man knew what he had to do. It had taken two years to set the stage for the drama. Now everything had to be done quickly. The drama was nearly over. They were ready now to march in.

. . . . . .

Inside the city, in the king's banquet hall, everyone waited, hardly daring to breathe. Daniel had been brought in, an old man now, in his seventies. But not a stooped cringing old man. A tall and healthy and noble old man. And very frightening.

"Are you that Daniel who was brought captive from Jerusalem by King Nebuchadnezzar?" The king's face was pale.

"I am," Daniel spoke quietly. He was the master. The king was the cringing one.

"I have heard that you have the Spirit of the holy God, and great wisdom and understanding. If you can tell me the meaning of this writing, you shall be clothed in scarlet and wear a gold chain about your neck and become the third ruler in the—"

"Keep your gifts for yourself. And give your rewards to another. But I shall tell you the meaning of the writing."

Belshazzar sank back into his chair, gaping. Everyone waited.

"O king," Daniel said, "God gave Nebuchadnezzar this mighty kingdom, and great power, so that all men trembled

107

before him. And when he became proud and obstinate, God took away his glory and power and drove him from his throne until he learned it is GOD who rules men's destinies. You knew all this, O Belshazzar, and yet you have raised yourself up against God and brought His holy vessels here and drunk wine from them while you praised YOUR gods, who neither see nor hear nor know anything. And the God who gave you life, you have not glorified. *And your very breath is in His hands.*"

Everyone waited.

"It's for this reason that these words are on the wall. MENE, MENE, TEKEL, UPHARSIN."

And waited.

"These words mean—"

And waited.

"Mene—God has judged your kingdom and has brought it to an end.

"Tekel—You have been weighed in the balances of God and have failed the test.

"Upharsin (Peres)—Your kingdom will be divided and given to the Medes and Persians."

The silence that followed was something you could almost *feel.* Then finally—"Give him the robe. Hang a gold chain about his neck. I declare him third ruler of the kingdom." But by now the king was babbling.

. . . . . .

Outside the city the marching orders were given. Under the gates. UNDER THE GATES! The army marched in on the bottom of the nearly dry riverbed. And the gates inside? Drunken guards? We don't know. At any rate, they were easily overcome. And Cyrus' soldiers crept through the streets, slithered like shadows around the palace, and into the palace—

. . . . . .

Up and down that huge banquet hall in the palace were devastation and death. King Belshazzar lay sprawled, face down, where he had fallen. And his blood flowed down the marble steps just as the wine had spilled down them an hour before.

.　.　.　.　.　.

Babylon awakened next morning from her stupor, her king dead. Cyrus had entered the city without a struggle.

The party was over.

Proud of Who You Are?
Or Who You THINK You Are?

Darius was. He was the general Cyrus had left to be king of Babylon.* He divided the country into states. And appointed governors over them. And appointed three presidents over the governors. One of them was Daniel. Who proved to be the most capable of all the governors. So

*Cyrus stayed awhile, then went off to conquer new worlds, leaving one of his generals, Darius, to rule Babylon.

Darius made plans to appoint Daniel over the entire empire as his administrative officer.

That's when the trouble began.

You know the story well. How the other governors became jealous. And how they went to the king with a proposition. That for thirty days no one could worship any god or ask anything of any man, except the king. And if anyone did, he would be thrown into the lions' den.

Naturally the proud Darius signed the law. And naturally Daniel continued to pray to his God. And naturally the king had Daniel thrown into the lions' den. And *super*naturally God delivered Daniel from the lions.

After which Darius decreed that: "Every one shall tremble and fear before the God of Daniel in every part of my kingdom. For his God is the living, unchanging God whose power shall never end."

Darius sure shaped up, and quick. He'd found out who he was. And it wasn't what he'd THOUGHT he was. Not by a long sight!

What Are You Proud Of?

Proud of what you've accomplished? Proud of what you have, though you did nothing to earn it? Proud of what you are (or think you are)? Or—and think—proud of being humble? It would be a shame to get everything else in your life nice and tidy, and then get tripped up by your pride.

A Brief Word with Your Conscience

YOU: I get the whole point, so don't jump on me. I never thought I was a hotshot.
CONSCIENCE: Never?

YOU: Okay, I'm a *little* proud in *some* areas. Small things. I'll work on it.

CONSCIENCE: You do that.

YOU: (DEFENSIVELY) But I don't mock God. Like Belshazzar. He drank wine out of the Lord's holy vessels.

CONSCIENCE: Well?

YOU: Okay I fool around a little in Sunday School.

CONSCIENCE: Isn't that a holy place?

YOU: I wish you'd go away and leave me alone.

CHAPTER 12

Why
Was I Born?

Portions of Esther, Chapters 1–8

"Nothing Ever Happens to Me!"

"I'm just a nobody and my life is dull and I never get any opportunities to do anything really exciting or important and—"

Ever catch yourself thinking this way? If you'd been born in a more important family, or rich, or of famous parents, then the opportunities for excitement would just pour in and everything would be jolly. But as things are, you don't have a chance!

There was a young girl in Persia who must have felt that way. Her name was Esther. And a rundown of her life made dull reading. She was a captive Jew. Her people had been among the prisoners taken from Jerusalem. She was an orphan. The only family she had was her older cousin Mordecai who had adopted her. Mordecai was a gatekeeper in the king's court, which was no great smash of a job, certainly not one to get Esther into the social whirl. Mordecai loved Esther, but the only life he could give her was a very ordinary one.

Then one day, out of the blue, a decree went forth from the palace—King Ahasuerus was searching for a new queen! The most beautiful girls in the realm were being sought, to be brought to the palace so the king could choose his queen from among them! Mordecai took Esther to the palace, warned her *not* to reveal that she was a Jew—and lo and behold, she was one of the maidens chosen to stay there, be dusted and polished, given a charm course, made into a grand lady, and eventually stand before the king as one of the contestants. (Sound like a fairy tale? It isn't; it really happened.)

And after a year of grooming and learning the manners of the royal court, she *did* stand before King Ahasuerus. And he *did* choose her. And she wound up with a crown on her head, queen of Persia!

Sound fantastic? Not really. For God had a plan for Esther's life, and this happened to be a part of it. No matter how ordinary you are, or think you are, God can do *extra*ordinary things with you.

"Where's My Reward?"

Well maybe we don't go around with our grubby little hands out every time we do something good. But sometimes there *is* a little twinge when there's no reward. We didn't want much, really. But just a little pat on the back? A little recognition? It does cross our minds. "The least they could do—"

Mordecai picked up all sorts of gossip at the king's gate.

It was there he discovered that two of the guards were plotting to *kill* the king. He got word to Esther, who "told

114

the king in Mordecai's name."* When it was investigated and found to be true, the men were caught and hanged. And did Mordecai get a reward? Or recognition? No, the event was written in the palace records, put on a shelf to gather dust, and forgotten. And there is no mention of Mordecai's griping about it. Of course we have no record of the possible twinges in his mind. All we know is, he saw his duty and he did it. Without fanfare.

"Who Wants to Look at Me?"

We'd die rather than admit that we like flattery and attention. And when we get it, we push it aside with a "Oh, it's nothing, really." It's when we *don't* get it that those crazy twinges start twinging again. Especially when any idiot can plainly see that we deserve it.

There was a noblemen in the king's court who was more conceited than noble. His name was Haman, he was chief of all the princes, he was next to the king himself, and he was an insufferable snob. Every time he went through the gate, the keepers and servants bowed low to him. It was their custom to bow before royalty as if they were worshiping a divine being. It was not Mordecai's custom to bow to anyone but God. Haman didn't notice this little slight until the other servants at the gate told him about it (he probably had his nose too high in the air). To put it mildly, he was furious. What? What? Who *is* this insolent fellow? How dare he? What? He's a Jew? Did you say a *Jew?*

"I Never Forget an Insult"

Don't you now? Well if you have a talent for remembering insults, it's a talent the Lord would just as soon you'd

*Read Esther 2:22.

bury. The smartest thing you can do is develop a good for-
gettery where insults are concerned. Some things just aren't
worth remembering.

The fact that Mordecai would not bow was like a burr in
Haman's hide. He simply could not forget it. That insolent
little man. So he was a Jew, was he? Well he could be destroyed. No, that was not enough. *All* the Jews should be
destroyed. Ah, that was better.

Haman decided to go to the king.

"I Just Twisted a Few Facts"

And did you, now? You didn't lie? You just left something
out? If this is your habit you'd do well to get over it before
you get someone in serious trouble. And "someone" could
be you.

Haman went to the king. And reported that there were
certain people scattered about who were not keeping the
king's laws. It was not profitable to tolerate them. If it
please the king, let it be decreed that they be destroyed.

Oh, yes, Haman would be glad to pay ten thousand talents of silver into the treasury. And oh, yes, trusty Haman would take care of everything. The king needn't bother his head about it. Haman neglected to say that these people were the captive Jews—thousands of them. And the king told Haman to write whatever decree was necessary, and gave him the royal signet ring to seal it. Now Haman had complete authority in the king's name to take care of the whole messy little business. Trusty ole Haman.

The decree that he sent out was a far cry from the little dealie he'd discussed with the king, "TO ALL OFFICIAL LEADERS: ON THE THIRTEENTH DAY OF THE MONTH OF ADAR, KILL AND DESTROY ALL JEWS, BOTH YOUNG AND OLD, LITTLE CHILDREN AND WOMEN: THEN SEIZE THEIR BELONGINGS."

It was a stunning blow. The Jews everywhere got into sackcloth and ashes, and mourned.

"Why Was I Ever Born?"

If you ever say this, and mean it as a complaint, stop in your tracks, give yourself a swift kick, and ask the Lord to forgive you. The only way you can say it is to leave out the "ever." And when you say "Why was I born?" You mean what is God's will for your life.

When Esther's attendants told her that Mordecai was out by the gate in sackcloth and ashes, she was frantic. What was wrong? She sent a messenger to Mordecai to find out. The answer that came back sent her spinning. It was a copy of Haman's decree. But the *personal* message from Mordecai put the weight of the world on Esther's shoulders. "Go to the king and beg him for the life of your people!"

It was impossible! No one—not even the queen could go to the king without being called, under penalty of death. Was Mordecai out of his mind? Esther sent a message back.

"All the king's servants . . . know that . . . [whoever] shall go
into the inner court to the king without being called shall be
put to death; there is but one law for him, except . . . to
whom the king shall hold out the golden scepter that he
may live. But I have not been called to come to the king
these thirty days!"*

And Mordecai's message came back: "Do not flatter yourself that you shall escape in the king's palace any more than
all the other Jews. For if you keep silent, God will find some
other way to deliver His people. And who knows but that
you have come to the kingdom *for just such a time as this?*"

And Esther, for the first time in her life, faced the question: "Why was I born?" She faced the answer, too. For the
message she sent back was: "Send the word out. Tell the
Jewish people not to eat or drink for three days. Tell them to
pray. I and my maids will also fast and pray. Then I will go
to the king. If I die, I die."

In that moment, Esther grew up.

· · · · · ·

Three days later a very frightened young girl stepped out
of the women's quarters of the palace—alone—and walked
slowly toward the court of the king. She was carefully and
beautifully dressed; the shadows under her eyes only en-
hanced her loveliness. She knew that unless the king raised
his golden scepter she would die. She walked toward the
throne like one in a dream. And then—

The king raised his golden scepter!

"What is your wish, Queen Esther, and what is your request? It shall be given you, even to half the kingdom."

Esther could barely find her voice, the relief was so great.
"If it seems good to the king, let the king—and Haman—
come this day to the dinner that I have prepared for the
king."

*Read Esther 4:11, "Amplified Bible."

"Send for Haman," the king told his attendants. "What Esther has asked shall be done."

Her request was granted! So far so good.

. . . . . .

"What is your request?" the king asked at dinner.

"If I have found favor in your sight," said Esther, "let the king and Haman come tomorrow and dine with me. Then I shall tell you my request."

And the king agreed. Things were going very well.

"I'll Get Even if It's the Last Thing I Do"

What? *You* said that? Have you *ever* said that? Watch it. Getting even is small business. Nasty. And messy. And dangerous. It just might *be* the last thing you will ever do. Forget it.

Haman left the palace that night so proud he was floating. But when he got to the gate, there was Mordecai, refusing to bow. Haman's spirits went down like a pricked balloon. That wretched Mordecai!

At home, Haman tried to blow himself up again by recounting all the honors that had been bestowed upon him.

"And so there you are," he told his wife and friends. "I have not only been promoted above any man in the kingdom, but I dined with the king and queen tonight and am invited to dine with them tomorrow night. My position is one of great honor."

Everyone beamed.

"Yet all this benefits me nothing, so long as I see Mordecai the Jew sitting at the king's gate!"* he bellowed.

Everyone frowned. Then:

"Have a gallows made!" they cried. "Speak to the king to-

*Esther 5:13, "Amplified Bible."

morrow. Have Mordecai hanged! Then go to your dinner with a merry heart."

Jolly idea. Haman decided to do it. In fact he went right out and gave the orders to have the gallows made at once. But he'd left one character out of the little drama. God.

Watch It—Your Little Plot Might Be Foiled

That very night the king couldn't sleep. And he ordered— of all things—that the book of records be read to him. The secretaries were yawning discreetly behind their hands as they read, but the king was never more wide awake. The night turned to dawn. They read on. And then— What was this? Mordecai saved the king's life? What? Had anything been done to honor him? No? What? Nothing?

"Who is outside standing in the court?" said the king.

"Haman," they said.

And sure enough, he was. He'd come to ask the king to have Mordecai hanged.

"Tell him to come in," said the king.

They did. "Tell me," said the king. "What shall be done to the man whom the king wishes to honor?"

And Haman puffed up almost to the bursting point.

"Naturally I'm the Best"

Well you don't come out and say it. But sometimes, do you *think* it? Naturally you should be class president, naturally you should be chosen for whatever. Naturally. Watch it. Bad business. Bad business indeed.

Naturally Haman thought he was the one the king wanted to honor. And naturally he thought up a dinger.

"Let royal clothes be brought which the king has worn, and the horse the king has ridden, and a royal crown set on his head. Then let one of the royal princes conduct him on horseback through the open square of the city and shout before him, This is the man the king delights to honor!" Haman was beside himself with pride. This was heady business.

"Good," said the king. "Do this to Mordecai the Jew. Make haste."

What was *this? Mordecai?* Mordecai the Jew, the little insignificant insubordinate insufferable intolerable *nobody?*

Good grief.

Haman started out of the room. But his knees were sagging. "And don't leave anything out that you have spoken," the king called after him.

Good grief. This was the end. He'd never make it. He knew he'd never make it, but he had to somehow.

Haman did as he was told. It was a great day for Mordecai. For Haman, it was the worst day he'd ever had in his life. The only saving factor was that he was dining with the king and queen that night.

"I Didn't Think It Would Turn out This Way"

No you never do, when you're making mischief. Everything is going nicely, and you think you are getting away with it, and then—

POW!

It was a nervous Haman who sat at the queen's table that night. What an awful turn things had taken! He could hardly get his mind on what was being said. How HAD things got so out of hand? His scalp prickled.

"What is your request?" the king was saying to Esther.

"If it please the king," Esther said, "let my life be saved, and the lives of my people. For we are sold, I and my people."

The king leaned forward. "Your people? Esther—"

"I am a Jew," she said quietly. But it filled the room like a thunderbolt.

Haman withered on his couch. Esther a Jew? The queen, a *Jew*? He was numb with shock. What a horrible development!

"If we'd been sold as slaves I would have held my tongue," Esther went on. "But we are sold to be destroyed, slain, and wiped out of existence. And our affliction could never be compared with the damage this will do to the king."

Haman almost slid under his couch.

"And who is he, and where is he, who dares to do this thing?" the king was saying.

"An enemy," said Esther. "The man who sits at this table. Haman."

The jig was up.

. . . . . .

The king put his goblet down on the table. Esther clasped her hands tightly together to stop their trembling. Haman's face sagged with fear. And they both watched the king. He got up, walked to the end of the room, came back. Then, as if the room could not contain his anger, disappeared through the half-open door, into the garden.

Haman turned to Esther and begged for his life. He was whimpering now. Not the proud Haman, favorite of the king.

The king came back through the garden door. And at the sight of him, one of the servants, who'd been glued to the spot at the unexpected drama, suddenly found his tongue.

"O king, there is a gallows standing by the house of Prince Haman. Gallows he had made for Mordecai, the man who saved your life."

Everyone waited. A moment. It seemed like a year.

The king nodded his head toward Haman, without even looking at him. "Hang him on it," he said.

The jig *was* up.

Haman didn't think it would turn out this way, either. But it did. All the mischief he'd planned came back upon his own head. Or in this case, around his neck.

"Why Was I Born?"

The rest? Just mopping up operations. The man who was willing to kill thousands of people because he hated one man, was hanged on the gallows he'd built for the man he hated. Irony? Yes, and purpose too, God's finger again, on the destiny of His people. They could not be destroyed, for they were His special people, through whom the Saviour was to come.

The law in the king's name could not be changed, but the order went out that the Jews *could fight back*. Which meant that now the Jews were under the care of the king. And who'd want to fight them seriously, under *those* conditions?

Instead of a slaughter, they celebrated a great feast to thank God and express their joy.*

Oh, yes. And Mordecai was given Haman's position.

And Esther? Well she sure knew *now* why she was born. Surely, she'd "come into the kingdom for just that purpose!"

"Why Was I Ever Born?"

Don't ever say that again. Just ask "Why was I born?" You have come into the kingdom for a purpose. Ask God what it is.

---

*It's still celebrated among the Jews today; it's called the Feast of Purim.

CHAPTER 13

Christians
Can't Be Sissies

Portions of Ezra, Nehemiah and Haggai

"I'm Zigging When I Should Be Zagging"

Off your course a little? Tacking when you should set
your rudder and sail straight? Wish you could get back to
God but the way seems hard? And long? Cheer up; you
have lots of company. You won't get back by moping
around. And you won't get back by thinking about it. The
first thing you do is *start*. Right now.

The Jews finally got back to Jerusalem and to God. It was
nip and tuck for awhile but they finally made it.

Remember Cyrus?* He's the chap who marched into Babylon on the dry riverbed. And as you know, Babylon was
laced with captive Jews. And wherever the Jews were, there

*Chapter 10.

were the oracles of God. Just how Cyrus happened upon the Word of God we don't know. Perhaps poring over the ancient records. Perhaps it was Daniel's doing. But in one of those scrolls were the words: *I am the LORD, that maketh all things. . . . That saith of Cyrus, He is my shepherd, and shall perform all my pleasure: even saying to Jerusalem, Thou shalt be built. . . . Thus saith the LORD to . . . Cyrus . . . I will go before thee . . . I will break in pieces the gates of brass . . . I will give thee the treasures of darkness, and hidden riches of secret places, that thou mayest know that I, [am] the LORD, which call thee by thy name . . . though thou hast not known me.**

You can believe that this brought Cyrus up with a bit of a jolt. For it had been written 200 years before he was born!

Anyhow the Bible tells us that "God stirred up Cyrus so that he made a proclamation, saying, 'The Lord hath charged me to build Him a house at Jerusalem. Who is there among you of his people? Go up to Jerusalem, build the house of the Lord, and God be with you.'"

He not only told the Jews they were free to go, but he passed the hat to see that they did not go empty-handed. Animals. Gold. Silver. Supplies. And the sacred vessels of the Temple!

And off they marched, singing songs. The journey was going to be a rough one, but at least they had made the start.

"I'm Off to a Start—a BUM Start"

And your "This Little Light of Mine—I'm Gonna Let It Shine"—is down to a sputter? Your intentions were good but you're running out of gas? Be patient. God is more anxious to help you than you are to help yourself.

*Isaiah 44:28; 45:1–4.

126

The first sight of the city of Jerusalem was enough to make the Jews' light sputter and go out. It lay in ruins—the Temple, the walls, the homes—everything that had once been so beautiful, now a heap of rubble.

The people set up shelters and dug in. They celebrated the Feast of the Tabernacles as their forefathers had done before them. They built an altar and offered burnt offerings to the Lord. They put their carpenters and masons to work on a foundation for the new Temple. But it was hard going.

"I Didn't Think There'd Be So Many Problems!"

Didn't you, now? Naturally you have problems. Satan isn't going to let you breeze through this without any problems. And God is going to *allow* you to have them to develop your spiritual muscles. So roll up your sleeves, dig in, and get going!

The Jews' biggest problem turned out to be the people of Samaria, who came down to see if they could get in on the act. Could they help rebuild the Temple? The Jews answered no, and the trouble began.

And trouble it was! The Samaritans wrote letters back to Persia. To Cyrus (who didn't get the message; he was off to war). To King Ahasuerus.* And to his successor, Artaxerxes. The letters were clever. "These people are rebellious. This city they are rebuilding is bad. If they rebuild this city and finish the walls, they will not pay you tribute—they will laugh in your face! they've rebelled before—they'll rebel again! And we do not want to see you discredited."

Ah, cagey, that.

And the letters did their deadly work. The answer came back: "Tell them to stop the work! Tell them the city is not to be rebuilt!"

*He was Esther's husband.

This was all the cue the Samaritans needed. The Bible tells us they troubled the Jews. And frustrated them. And terrified them. And hired counselors against them.

The work stopped. The poor little light was barely sputtering.

"Aren't I to Get Any Encouragement?"

When God gives you problems, He usually gives you some encouragement to go along with them. Even if there seems to be no human encouragement, there is always the knowledge that He is with you, and knows what He's doing, no matter *how* the whole wretched business seems to you.

And how did God give the Jews encouragement? He gave them two prophets for those dark days. Haggai. And Zechariah. He told them through Haggai: "Build the Temple and I will be pleased with you and will bless you, says the Lord."* And He told them through Zechariah: "It shall not be by might, nor by power, but by My Spirit, says the Lord. The hands of Zerubbabel had laid the foundations of this Temple and his hands shall finish it."

"The Problems Were Too Much—I Fell on My Face Again!"

Well pick yourself up. You are not alone. It happens to the nicest people. And it happened to the Jews.

Those dark days had taken their toll. While the work was being held up, they slipped *down*. And *down*. They did finally finish the Temple all right. But they also began to marry the heathen outside. They, in short, "fell on their

*Read Haggai 1:2–11.

face." Things were in a sorry mess. And the walls were still in ruins.

"What Bible?"

Yes. What Bible indeed. Sometimes we act as if we'd never heard of it. The Bible that stays on your lap, closed, during meetings. The Bible that lays on your shelf and gathers dust. God wants you to get in it. *In* it. And to get in it, you have to open it. See?

Well, God "opened the Bible" for those poor misguided discouraged Jews. In the form of a man named Ezra. Another decree was issued back in Persia: That Ezra would take another group of captive Jews back to Jerusalem. With unlimited authority for spending funds from the royal treasure for the support of the Temple. And Ezra was a priest! He could trace his ancestry back to Aaron! And he was well-versed in the Word of God!

God was certainly doing *His* part. But the Jews? Ezra, when he got to Jerusalem, plunged into a sea of trouble. Heathen wives and husbands. With their children speaking a gibberish that was half their own language and half the sacred Hebrew. Trouble, trouble, everywhere. Ezra tried to lead them back to a closer walk with God. He "opened the Bible" to them (as your Sunday School teacher "opens the Bible" to you) but they were awfully hard of hearing. The people were sluggish. The work was slow. Years went by. And the walls were still in ruins. Nasty business.

"What a Sorry Mess My Life Is!"

Your "walls" are down? And you're too discouraged to clean up the mess? Come *on* now. You don't actually believe this. Nothing's too messy to clean up, when you have God on your side. Buck up!

Those poor Jews were in about as sorry a mess as you can imagine. It was the "darkest hour" before the dawn. But the "dawn" did come. In the person of a young man named Nehemiah.

Nehemiah was a cupbearer in the palace of the king of Persia. It was his duty to taste the wine before giving it to the king. Now a cupbearer in Persia was a royal favorite, with privilege and power and wealth. One to be envied. You really had to be *something* to be a cupbearer.

There isn't time to tell the whole story here, but Nehemiah heard of the plight of the Jews and what a sorry mess they'd got themselves into, and it plunged him into the darkest gloom. When he told the king about it, the king gave him a "furlough" to go to Jerusalem and see if he could clean up the mess. With money. And letters of credit. And a military escort!

"But This Is Hopeless!"

Naturally you think your particular case is hopeless. You think nobody, but *nobody,* ever went through *this* before. News for you. Lots of people have. And no case is hopeless, with God.

There is no tale so sad as the tale of Nehemiah's inspection of Jerusalem. At night. With only a few men with him. Sad, sad.

He went out by the Valley Gate toward the Dragon's Well. To the Dung Gate. Over to the Fountain Gate. To the King's Pool. Now there was no place for the beast he was riding on to walk; the rubble was too great. He walked. Up by the brook Kedron. And back. In by the Valley Gate. Everything was broken down; everything was in ruins. Everything was hopeless, hopeless, hopeless . . .

But did he give up? No!

He went back to the officials of the town and said:

130

"I'm Going to Try Again!"

Yahweeeee! Whaahoooo! "I'm going to try again!" Are there any sweeter words under heaven? God sure likes to hear them! Well, what are you *waiting* for?

"LET US RISE AND BUILD!" the people cried back. And they did. They plunged in, and did build, falling over each other in their enthusiasm to get the job done. Volunteers from every profession, every walk of life.

"I'll take this portion of the wall!" "I'll take the Fish Gate!" "I and my sons will take this part!" "The Valley Gate!" "The Dung Gate!" "The Fountain Gate!"

Side by side!

And they built and they built, side by side, calling out to each other for encouragement.

"I Tried Again—And I STILL Have Problems!"

Of course you have! But don't give up now, just as you've got up your steam! Keep the old steam up!

The Jews' problems were all wrapped up in a man by the name of Sanballat. Governor of Samaria. And was *he* a rascal! (There's always *someone*.)

"People Are Sneering at Me!"

Your feeble efforts are making you look like some sort of a wobbly-bobbly? Nobody thinks you are really making it? Oh, come *on* now. God knows you're making it. Forget about people.

Sanballat and his men gave the Jews a *terrible* time.

"What are the feeble Jews doing?" they sneered. "If a fox climbed up on that wall, he'd break it!"*

But Nehemiah told the Jews, "Don't be afraid. God will fight for us."

"But People Are Plotting Against Me!"

Well sometimes you imagine they are, and sometimes they really *are*. So what? Is not God still on your side? Carry on! Watch and *pray!*

The wall was half up. The Samaritans were by now ready to fight. They came against the Jews, armed, ready for the kill. But half of those Jews armed themselves with swords, and they laid stones with one hand while they held a sword in the other! And the other half stood watch! Yes! With swords! They didn't stop to take their clothes off! They meant BUSINESS!

"But My Scoffers Are Trying to Trap Me!"

Sure they are. Tying to get you to "talk it over." Hear *their* side. Don't fall for it. It's pure rubbish.

Sanballat tried that game on Nehemiah. "Come, let us meet together in one of the villages on the plain; I want to talk to you." Nehemiah didn't bite. He knew that Sanballat meant nothing but trouble. "I'm doing a great work for the Lord," he shot back. "Why should I stop and come down to talk with you?"

He was sure smart.

"My Scoffers Are Calling Me a Would-be Hot-shot"

So they think you're being "spiritual" and "goody-goody" for what you can get out of it? Ridiculous. Ignore them.

*Read Nehemiah 4:2,3.

Sanballat sent Nehemiah a letter accusing him of building up that wall so he would eventually be king. A hotshot! "You've made *that* one up in your own mind," said Nehemiah. "Forget it." But he thought, "Frighten me? So my hands will be weak? And my work will not get done? O Lord, strengthen my hands!" What did he do? He prayed, of course.

Good idea.

"I'm Trying, but, Boy, Sometimes They Frighten Me!"

Sure. They sometimes shock you out of your senses. Nobody's going to kill you, but they sure can threaten to mow you down. Kill off your popularity. Your reputation with the gang. Just *mow you down*. Sometimes you get it from your enemies. Sometimes you get if from your so-called friends.

Sanballat hired a false prophet to give this line to Nehemiah. "Hide in the Temple," he warned. "Hide in the Temple, for they are coming to kill you, at night they are coming to kill you!"

"I should be afraid?" said Nehemiah. "I should run? You're a PHONY. You want me to run scared? So you can laugh at me later? IIa. No deal." And in spite of all the threats and all the problems, the people built and built and built. Until the wall was finished—in 52 days!

"Boy, I'm Going to MAKE It!"

Sure you will. You've had problems, people have sneered at you, plotted against you, scoffed at you, called you a hotshot, frightened you—BUT YOU'RE GOING TO MAKE IT.

133

And so did they. And did they ever have a feast day!

And after the feast, they gathered in the gate and they asked Ezra to read to them from the Word of God. And he read from morning till noon. And they stood and listened, from morning till noon! And then they bowed down and worshiped the Lord and wept for their sins.

"I'm Sorry; What Do I Do Now?"

Well blow your nose and dry your eyes. Don't just stand there bawling. You've come through!

Ezra told the people to feed the poor, divide their plenty, HELP people. And they did.

"I'm Spinning Along Fine Now; Can't I Relax?"

Your so-called "friends"—and your enemies—have admitted defeat? You have, at long last and after many battles, been proved right? So now you can relax? Well *don't*.

Bad business.

"Now when all our enemies heard of it, all the nations around us feared and fell far in their own esteem, for they saw that this work was done by our God," says Nehemiah.

BUT.

When the wall was built, he set a WATCH ON GUARD. He was taking no chances. Don't you. Watch and pray. Your watch IS prayer. You've won the victory? Don't let down now!

Christians can't be sissies. It's a fighting business.

. . . . . .

The people of Judah had at last come home. The long long struggle was over.

Over? No, there were problems ahead. There would always be problems ahead. This is the way it was with them. And this is the way it is with you. This is the way it will always be.

"What's God Trying to Do with ME?"

This is God's way with you. He must allow you to have problems; it's the only way He can "grow you up." And He has spent so much time planning for you, thinking about you, watching you being formed, then being born, a living being. How His heart is set upon you! And what plans He has for you! You are *you*, unique, there is nobody else like you in all the world.

As you set this book down,* think about yourself and God, and of His great personal love for you. And ask Him what He has in mind to do for *your* life.

You can put yourself in no better hands.

*And I hope you've read it.